Detoxing American Schools

Other Works by This Author

America's Sex Culture: It's Impact upon Teacher Student Relationships Today (2020)
The Age of Teacher Shortages: Reasons, Responsibilities, Reactions (2019)
Generación Z: La Generación con Derechos (2019)
Assaulted: Violence in Schools and What Needs to Be Done (2018)
The Teacher Exodus: Reversing the Trend and Keeping Teachers in the Classrooms (2018)
The Entitled Generation: Helping Teachers Teach and Reach the Minds and Hearts of Generation Z (2017)
Helping Parents Understand the Minds and Hearts of Generation Z (2017)
Common Sense Education: From Common Core to ESSA and Beyond (2016)
The Wrong Direction for Today's Schools: The Impact of Common Core on American Education (2015)
Teacher-Student Relationships: Crossing into the Emotional, Physical, and Sexual Realms (2013)
It Should Never Happen Here: A Guide for Minimizing the of Child Abuse in Ministry (1997)

Detoxing American Schools

From Social Agency to Academic Urgency

Ernest J. Zarra III

ROWMAN & LITTLEFIELD
Lanham • Boulder • New York • London

Published by Rowman & Littlefield
A wholly owned subsidiary of The Rowman & Littlefield Publishing Group, Inc.
4501 Forbes Boulevard, Suite 200, Lanham, Maryland 20706
www.rowman.com

6 Tinworth Street, London, SE11 5AL, United Kingdom

Copyright © 2020 by Ernest J. Zarra III

All rights reserved. No part of this book may be reproduced in any form or by any electronic or mechanical means, including information storage and retrieval systems, without written permission from the publisher, except by a reviewer who may quote passages in a review.

British Library Cataloguing in Publication Information Available

Library of Congress Cataloging-in-Publication Data

ISBN 978-1-4758-5263-9 (cloth : alk. paper)
ISBN 978-1-4758-5264-6 (paper : alk. paper)
ISBN 978-1-4758-5265-3 (electronic)

This book is dedicated to Elya and Jonathan,
two millennials whose lives and accomplishments
have helped this baby boomer father to understand what
it means to have ineffable pride for one's children.

Contents

	List of Tables	ix
	Preface	xi
	Acknowledgments	xxi
Chapter 1	America's Toxic History	1
Chapter 2	Neo-Toxic Culture	25
Chapter 3	Trauma and Drama	57
Chapter 4	Are You a Toxic Teacher?	83
Chapter 5	Toxic Teachings	105
Chapter 6	Detoxing American Schools	137
	Index	159
	About the Author	167

List of Tables

Table 3.1 Addictions in American Society   67
Table 5.1 Toxic Issues in American Schools   109
Table 6.1 Is Your School Toxic?   139

Preface

Not every school is toxic. Not every teacher is toxic, and certainly not every teaching is toxic. But we humans have toxic tendencies and, given the right combination of people and circumstances, the results become quite unpredictable. When partisan groups gather around issues for which they are impassioned, the dynamics of belief, persona, and expression intersect. Add in ways Americans communicate online, and this emotional intersection can quickly become explosive and toxic.

Lately, with all the discussion and concerns about trauma and trauma-informed teaching—as well as school violence, bullying of students and teachers, unruly parents, and the highly partisan political environment in which the nation finds itself—there can be little doubt that America is in the midst of toxic fallout. Since schools are a reflection of culture, these institutions are where reflections of disrepair become revelations of opportunities, sometimes emphasized by rogue teacher-activists and targeted school curriculum.

There is justification today for the concerns of many parents and teachers. Many observe unwelcome changes becoming established in schools. Psychological theories, mixed with social causes and political forces, often prompt insularity and partisan marginalization in culture. Since schools are grounds for cultural germination, they are targets for change.

American culture has always been prompted and affected by people with national voices. With each of these voices there are choices. However, today's American culture has veered into territory that goes beyond only one *voice*. The past is being drowned out, and panic-stricken alarmists tell us the future looks bleak. So younger generations live in the present as if there is no past worthy of afterthought and no future hope. But these are toxic positions—the likes of which are causing today's students serious apprehension about their future.

As a result of the Internet and social media, some voices have become toxic icons, and these toxic icons have established toxic followings. The result today is that followings are not settling for anything less than a modern-day tyrannical power play, the result of which is the punishment of dissenters. These icons affect what is taught in schools and how curriculum is shaped.

Schools have become places of social agency, pressing activism for a fringe percentage of Americans. The toxic part is that there is the expectation that all students must come to accept cultural beliefs without question. In efforts to ensure this expectation is met, some advocates have made certain to identify their social causes as academic curriculum. In other words, the identity of education has been remade into a social agency with targeted outcomes.

This approach is a far cry from schools being the academic hubs of learning and critical thinking, which most parents expect schools to focus on for their children. It is this clash of expectations that results in exacerbating polarization and superfluous toxicity.

There are no better examples in many public schools of social agency than the iconic voices of activism focused on the end of the world through climate change alarmism. In addition, other voices include LGBTQ+ inclusion theories, schools' modern sex-education courses, restorative justice programs, and others. The voices stand in contrast to those who disagree and are subject to practices of intolerance levied upon those with outcries of dissent.

Another major example of toxicity is the vast gulf between political parties and the horrendous incivilities that are manifest because of rhetoric. The inability of hyper-partisans to listen and the rampant emotions that sometimes fuel violent actions are becoming all too commonplace in culture. The nation is stalemated. There is no reason to listen to either side's political or social views, especially when each side seeks empowerment to tyrannize and punish the other politically.

What could be more toxic than families that send their children to schools and colleges only to return with beliefs, practices, and identities that are toxic to their traditional family and upbringing? American culture is toxic at its core and national unity seems beyond reach. Then, there are the schools: the thermostats of toxicity in culture.

Students are the next generation of budding practitioners of knowledge and new expressions. Students are being encouraged to become civically involved. However, the slant by which they are being encouraged is decisively unilateral and unidirectional. This is why it is critically important to think carefully about the people and influences that plant this knowledge and teach these expressions.

A by-product of the direction education is going leaves students open to ideologies and practices that would seemingly encourage students to act with dissent over agreement. Consequently, dissent has been weaponized, and its empowerment is the doctrinaire foundation of toxicity under the guises of nationalism, equal rights, and identity.

The Importance of This Book

Teachers are culture changers. They now actively affirm personal beliefs as advocates. Some teachers select curriculum that is outside the parameters of their schools and districts in order to promote a noxious level of activism, which is intentionally coupled with social-emotional conditioning.

Teachers today are more vocally partisan in creating more toxic classrooms in the process. This book is important for three major reasons, as it (1) examines American neo-culture, (2) identifies the general directions it is taking American society, and (3) analyzes specific toxic teachings that presently captivate American schools.

The notion that public schools are the same today as they were just a decade ago is an erroneous idea. Today's schools and students are vastly different. Schools are now places of advocacy that just a decade ago would have been considered aberrant and off-limits in classrooms. Social media has helped to break down morality of the past and provides tempting new viewpoints for today's students. Therefore, what was wrong a generation ago is fast becoming a norm. These norms are exacerbating levels of toxicity in American schools. Another reason for this book is to lay out a compelling case that toxicity does not emerge from one side of belief systems only.

Today's students are *intoxicated* with emotional self-expression and identity. One of the most toxic things that has emerged within American culture is the belief that biology and science have little to do with what people choose to believe about themselves. They are enamored with not understanding who they are and are open to qualified confusion. It is as if their confusion is an intoxicant. This places some students at odds with their parents, which some seem to celebrate.

To their parents' chagrin, students have listened to culture voices that proclaim they should look deep within their confusion and allow the confusion to work itself out over time and this will help to determine their own personal destiny. This appears to be a natural fit for Gen Z and some millennials. The fact that Gen Z and many millennials have had many things handed to them without great struggle means they are already confused about their place in the real world.

To many adults, schools have become intentional in creating confusion in the lives of their children. This book is very important because it points out that confusion does not add to clarity and that schools ought not to be places to celebrate this confusion.

There is no better example than high school graduates envisioning themselves as college students and athletes, and parents making those things happen by paying money for the student's assumed identity. This book will help to reason through today's school culture by providing insights to some of the causes and effects of the cultural stupor that characterizes today's generation.

Reasons for Writing This Book

American schools have become places of political activism and direct moral influence.

There is the complaint that teachers do not have enough time to teach academics because of so many other nonacademic program elements thrust upon them. But there are other areas that eat up classroom time, and these are addressed within the pages of this book.

As the old saying goes, students are going to feel all sorts of empathy for others out of work but become depressed for their own unemployment. One reason for writing this book is to point out that academics can be recovered if schools allow teachers to focus on five basic considerations:

1. Spending less time shaping a students' mind-sets and teaching math and reading sets
2. Bringing in exciting topics that ready students for the next level of education, that cause growth for all and do not undercut traditional family values for the sake of political correctness
3. Ceasing activism or advocacy toward one issue or one group at the expense of fairness and equity for all
4. Steering clear of the moral and social issues of gender, sex, and identity and viewing students as humans with academic as well as social needs
5. Understanding that, by focusing so much on inclusion that an environment of exclusion is created, results in a toxic environment of its own

The Possibility of Moderation

Schools have become intolerant of beliefs and practices that were mainstream and normed for schools for decades. The onset of lawsuits have marginalized Americans' freedom of speech and expression. Even holidays have been called into question and dropped in favor of celebrations that have become toxic in and of themselves.

Given these realities, what are the chances that progressives and traditionalists can ever agree on changes that need to occur in education while leaving alone the traditions that have long defined our national identity? Recent trends indicate that public education is more entrenched today in advancing political and social progressivism. Most unwelcome are retreats from advancement, and notions of status quo are rejected as draconian, bigoted, and racist.

Pejoratives are used today toward those whose positions are polar opposites of change agents. These pejoratives add to the coarseness of American culture and do little to assist in moderation of disagreements. In fact, disagreements today result in battles on the Internet and on cable news programs, where destruction of people and their positions have usurped the ability and desire for impassioned debate.

People are literally expressing their desires for death of adversaries over disagreements today. Evidence this by the statements of politicians and entertainers calling for boycotts, violence, and even assassination of certain disagreeable political leaders. In two decades, the United States has gone from fighting terrorism to electing supporters of the very terrorists who perpetrated the horrific events on September 11, 2001.

People tend to think that toxicity is the result of a majority foisting its will upon a minority. Certainly, that is one of the concerns regarding tyranny. In twenty-first-century America, laws tend to empower numeric minorities with arrogance and then make certain the empowered can brandish their partisan successes with impunity at the expense of moderation.

A minority that resorts to the same tactics previously practiced by a majority is vengeful and just as toxic. It is true that the eye-for-an-eye approach to legislation and enforcement of laws only results in a blind society. Forcing people to *see things our way* under those conditions is hardly a tolerant thing to do.

America has learned many lessons from its less than perfect past. It is just as intolerant today to practice similar imperfections of the past by force of law. Yet today's intolerance goes a step further. There is intolerance and disallowance of many of the traditions and values of others with whom there are mere disagreements. Unfortunately, disagreements are now equivalent to hatred, resulting in volatile name-calling and further marginalization.

The Risk

While writing about toxic environments in schools, an author risks being called a toxic agitator or worse yet summarily marginalized and dismissed because of disagreement. Analyzing and critiquing toxicity in society and across cultures will no doubt be deemed an aggression and toxic in its own right. This is most unfortunate that people cannot gain understanding through dialogue, which is what this book is intended to accomplish.

One person's toxicity is another person's disagreement. As long as professionals are not allowed to disagree without being shut down, there will only be an increase of toxic retribution. Truly, if ideas cannot stand on their merits or philosophies cannot be challenged without acrimony, true education is stunted. Unfortunately, this is the place to which we are taking our nation's students. Furthermore, this is the kind of factional power that the Founding Fathers, such as James Madison, and other Federalists warned against.

Opinions vary on the issues addressed in this book, and precisely, because education is of paramount importance, these issues must be addressed. The opinions taken by this author should be weighed no differently than those of professors and educators who consider themselves more progressive. The argument that something is true because an authority says so or because a person is a self-styled expert should be able to be challenged. I welcome the respectful comments and challenges regarding the ideas presented within the pages of this book.

Whether it is racism, toxic masculinity, cultural appropriation, or anything else that informs the basis of toxic environments in schools, this book will provide greater understanding into the toxicity that exists in American schools and culture as well as help willing teachers and parents to move toward refocusing on academics with the urgency our nation's children deserve.

The Inspiration for This Book

There are many traditional American values that are cherished in this nation because they are good and wholesome. The loss of these traditional values in American culture has consequences. It has led to a more toxic environment for students, teachers, and the American family. This book is inspired by the possibilities of civil agreement and the ability to learn from those with whom there are disagreements.

Interestingly, the toxicity between marginalized adult parties in schools inspires me to address the toxins we are creating in the psyches and brains of a generation of students. One cannot think of toxicity without also bringing the element of poisoning into the mix. How is it that young minds can be poisoned by belief? They can be poisoned by being told things that are not true and not corrected when there is error.

It appears that the once-taught Golden Rule has been turned upside down in American culture. For example, rather than *Do unto others as you would have them do unto you* is now more relevant as *Do unto others before they do unto you*. The latter also comes with modern cultural axioms that something is wrong only if one gets caught in the act of wrongdoing. These examples show the need to be corrected and also demonstrate toxic errors in thinking.

Another example of a basic belief that needs to be corrected is winning at all cost. Winning today seems more important than losing with pride and ethics. The ends justify the means today, which is a far cry from many of the values of our forebears and what was taught even in logic classes. It is purely toxic to allow children the freedom of speech to accuse people of wrongdoing or call them names to sully their reputations in order to quiet people with whom they disagree. These are also examples of toxic thought as well as practice.

When culture lurches one direction or another, there are victors and also-rans. When the also-rans are the majority of the nation, it is incumbent upon the victors to assimilate. I am inspired by those who practice moderation and understanding that cultural vestiges die hard deaths. I am equally inspired by mutual respect and the willingness to accept newly defined values. Likewise, I am inspired by those who claim to be traditionalists because common sense is also a value that Americans have come to accept and practice.

On balance, I am inspired by differences and similarities and how these play out in the lives of the next generation of students in schools. Will America ever return to a place of unity and leave behind the marginalized toxicity that has now become both ensconced and gregarious?

Academic urgency must return to American schools and place social and partisan emphases into less of a prominent role in public schools if students are going to become anything more than socially engineered safe-spacers, intolerant of dissent and emotive as adults.

The Structure of This Book

The general structure of the book is designed to accomplish the following tasks:

- Place many of the more common toxic topics found in America's public school into one volume

- Inform teachers in training about the state of toxicity in American schools and the challenges of managing today's public school classrooms
- Illustrate the impacts of teachers' actions in the classrooms, and question which actions are more appropriate for students' academic outcomes

The following six chapters are written to accomplish the above tasks.

Chapter 1 addresses America's toxic history by illuminating some of the nation's more infamous past events. There is a general discussion on the issues and concerns associated with factions. There is an examination of *the cult of individuals* in American society and the impact this has had on schools in the past. The changes in education policy and the ways education has been affected by societal changes are also included in chapter 1. The chapter includes sections on past and present toxic inputs into American culture, including outcomes of many Supreme Court cases, as well as how the terrorist attack on September 11, 2001, changed American culture.

Chapter 2 analyzes the rise of a new toxic America. This chapter includes examinations of politics and political figures, and the use of mind-numbing all-purpose pejoratives. Twenty-first-century toxic issues are addressed, and examples are used throughout the chapter. In addition to politics, this chapter reports on religion, marriage and family, sexual and gender identities, state laws, free speech, sports, and a range of other topics that fit the new toxic environment affecting both American culture and our schools.

Chapter 3 examines the *traumas and dramas* associated with toxic environments in American culture. Students today come to school with so very many traumatic experiences from home that they are *toxic time bombs*. This chapter looks into some of these traumas, such as violence, drug abuse, addictions, and special needs. It also questions whether American schools should be the agencies to deal with society's ills over being places of academics first. Some of the dramas include higher education, social organizations, and activism and ideologies, among others. Chapter 3 also includes a helpful table for teachers and parents to understand the current addictions facing students in American schools.

Chapter 4 zeroes in on the teacher. The chapter title asks *Are You a Toxic Teacher?* Throughout the chapter, toxic teachers are provided as examples, and the modern public school teacher is encouraged to look within to see whether there are things being taught to students that are triggering harm below the surface. Teachers are also challenged to examine the levels of influence they have in students' lives and to question their personal biases. The chapter also provides information for administrators on ways to handle toxic teachers.

Chapter 5 details many specific toxic teachings that are found in America's public schools and how these teachings are being received by the public. The chapter begins with toxic indicators that are embedded in most toxic teachings. It continues by asking about teaching methods and whether these methods might be causes of added toxicity. Topics such as educating the whole child, toxic masculinity, sex and gender, curriculum, and effects of toxicity are found detailed in the chapter. Chapter 5 includes a table of examples of toxic issues in American public schools, each of which is categorized by (1) highly toxic, (2) moderately toxic, or (3) slightly toxic.

Chapter 6 digs into the framework and interworkings of toxic schools. The ways boys and girls are treated in schools speaks volumes about toxic schools. The school culture is indicative of the health or the toxicity of a campus. The relationships between teachers, students, and parents are gauges of school health. Administrators are also challenged in this chapter to examine their leadership and the culture they have allowed to develop on campus. The school leader sets the tone for a healthy relational campus or a poisonous one. Ideas about how to bring schools out of toxicity are included in this chapter. Chapter 6 includes a helpful checklist for administrators and teachers to self-evaluate whether the schools at which they work are toxic environments.

Acknowledgments

I am blessed to have been a classroom teacher, coach, college professor, author, and professional development presenter throughout my lifetime. Each of these could not have been accomplished without many years of study, work, and reliance on the dedication of people in my life. But worth more than all of these accomplishments combined are the relationships with people who have changed my life at pivotal points along the way.

Some of the people who have mentored me both personally and professionally are no longer with us on the planet. But I have no doubt that I shall see them again. I have far too many to list and so very many to thank.

From the professors of my undergraduate years at Northeastern Bible College (where I came to understand the spiritual side of life), to the individual tutelage of Drs. John Warwick Montgomery and Dallas Willard and their impacts in my life and faith—and to the public school colleagues and college faculty—all of whom I adore to this day, I owe more than I could ever repay. Please accept this book as evidence of your impacts in my life.

Parents and students over the years have kept watchful eyes on American culture, and their alerts have prompted more than a little concern. So I want to thank the culture watchers and societal guardians for their input into this book. Your contributions continue to make all the difference in the world for our children and grandchildren. Your personal admiration and professional attention have served as motivational incentives for this book. All of us agree that the nation is heading is an unwise and different direction. Please know that I stand united with you at this time and that I am blessed and honored to work together with you for the sake of our nation.

As always, I acknowledge my wife—a new grandmother—and my Pacific Northwest gym partner. Suzi's support in allowing the time needed to accomplish this undertaking is never taken for granted. She is the best lifelong partner a man could ever hope for. Her love and commitment to her family is second to none, and her sounding-board thoughts and critiques have helped to shape certain segments of this book.

Last, I would like to acknowledge my mother and her choices in those early days; she continues to make me smile and press onward. Thanks, Mom. I will always love you, and I will always be your son.

CHAPTER ONE

~

America's Toxic History

> Vanilla and chocolate lovers do not disapprove of, or even dislike, each other, but Democrats and Republicans do. A preference does not need an argument, but a partisan contention does need one, indeed consists in one.
>
> —Harvey Mansfield[1]

> Ninety-nine in a hundred of what are called educated men are in this condition; even of those who can argue fluently for their opinions. Their conclusion may be true, but it might be false for anything they know: they have never thrown themselves into the mental position of those who think differently from them, and considered what such persons may have to say; and consequently they do not, in any proper sense of the word, know the doctrine which they themselves profess.
>
> —John Stuart Mill, *On Liberty*[2]

Toxicity in one form or another has always been a part of American history. In fact, there is an element of truth in the statement that toxicity is part of every people group and every nation of the world. Consequently, America is no exception to this toxicity. We are all, as humans—whatever the history and whatever the nation—toxic on many levels.

When it comes to American politics, some of the presidential races of the past were punishing and full of vitriol and anger. In terms of social struggles, the same is true. Sometimes, anger leads to violence, which eventually marks these types of struggles. Even religion can be toxic, for a variety of internal and external reasons, not the least of which is the joint deistic and Christian heritage upon which the United States was founded.[3]

As a means of context, as with most societies, toxic climates can be aligned to certain toxic historical actions and events. In the United States, the nation's list would include slavery, religious persecution, the establishment of the colonies, the Civil War, the Emancipation Proclamation, Reconstruction, World Wars I and II, the Korean and Vietnam Wars, Jim Crow Laws, assassinations of political and religious leaders, voting rights for women, racial struggles, abortion, same-sex marriage, and the list could go on. These are major events and ultimate turning points in American history.

As long as free people are able to express their disenchantment of the limitations of their freedom, and challenge status quo—as well as proclaim a moral and legal high grounds by use of a court system and the media—there will be toxicity in culture. From religion and politics, to economic and social actions, toxicity has always been with us and will continue. To phrase it differently, one could maintain that, as long as there are isms in culture, there will be spasms within that culture. Times change, and these changes in society are often first observed within cultural groups. In short order, each eventually ripples into the core of America's public schools.

Factions of the Past

Factions are nothing new. What is new is the name of the faction and how it handles its advocacy. James Madison, in *Federalist #10*, "warned against factions, which he regarded as the greatest scourge of democratic government. Two centuries later, the terminology is different but its normative resonance remains the same. Rather than employ the now-quaint word 'faction,' modern commentators are more likely to speak of special interests, vested interests, lobbies, pressure groups, and (in certain cases and with particular scorn) single-issue groups."[4]

Madison's definition of the term *faction* amounts to "a number of citizens, whether amounting to a majority or a minority of the whole, who are united and actuated by some common impulse of passion, or of interest, adverse to the rights of other citizens, or to the permanent and aggregate interests of the community."[5]

The Founding Fathers, those who generally took sides politically, were also members of their own factions and were able to understand what motivates people toward action. Madison addresses these motivations and remedies:

> There are again two methods of removing the causes of faction: the one, by destroying the liberty which is essential to its existence; the other, by giving to

every citizen the same opinions, the same passions, and the same interests. It could never be more truly said than of the first remedy, that it was worse than the disease. Liberty is to faction what air is to fire, an aliment without which it instantly expires. But it could not be less folly to abolish liberty, which is essential to political life, because it nourishes faction, than it would be to wish the annihilation of air, which is essential to animal life, because it imparts to fire its destructive agency.[6]

One reason factions have always caught the wary political eye is that they tend to become highly partisan. Each seeks "to prevail over its opposite, but not merely to prevail in the sense of winning a game, winning once at the end of the game. It wants to rule the whole society, including its opponent, and it wants to do so by imposing its rule, which means its set of rules. To rule is to rule by a principle that rules, by continuing to rule."[7] For example, the pro-life or pro-choice contention wants not just a single victory but, like the victory of the pro-choice contention in *Roe v. Wade*, one that establishes its principle as ruling the whole. "A party is a part of the whole that wants to rule the whole. Its contention is a claim to rule, a justification of its rule against that of its opponent or opponents."[8]

Passion

Factions in the twenty-first century are based on "intensity of feeling in the pursuit of one's interest."[9] However, Madison's "interest and passion are distinguished as two separate impulses, and passion is given greater power and scope. . . . Different interests are expressed in different opinions, not only regarding property but also religion and government, and these are put forward with 'zeal,' resulting in 'mutual animosities.'"[10]

There is no disagreement that Madison incorporated the political philosophy of John Locke and followed his teachings. Madison's ideas begin with the premise that "individuals who do not belong to a whole . . . must create one by consent"[11] and that "ambition by itself may not be a good thing, but in a competition of 'supplying, by opposite and rival interests, the defect of better motives,' the result is good."[12] Therefore, to Madison, the classic "difference between party and faction comes down to the difference between good and bad ambition."[13]

Ambition

Conflicts in classrooms do not necessarily have to be equated with toxic ambitions. However, more often than not, the two are conflated as one. Sometimes, conflicts are the results of ambitions to reshape culture, which can be accomplished through indoctrination and revolution. For example, there are some similarities between the religious movements of a few decades ago and the current radical, social, and identity movements. Anyone having come through the competitive religious movement of the 1970s, with the influx of Eastern religions and the rapid spread of American cults, may perceive a similar pattern that has emerged in culture and is impacting American public schools.

For starters, schools are being used today to spread modern ideologies with ambition to convert students. For example, states such as California, Illinois, and Massachusetts have radically altered their curriculum to reflect values that are contrary to historical, traditional, moral, and family values. Elections have consequences, and states with majorities of progressive elected officials are proposing swift changes to school curriculum.

Religious cults of the recent past ensnared followers with their own new brands of toxic teachings. Many of these teachings have morphed into building better humans by incorporating an exclusive type of toxic elitism. Each of these is challenging to classrooms all over the nation. False doctrines and neo-orthodoxies still ensnare the same way today but are packaged just a bit differently.

People tend to think that something new and creative is worthy of elevated status. The same is true in education. Most disturbing are those efforts that indoctrinate children to ideas and hold families hostage to accomplish cultural changes. As a means of reflection, who can forget the following personalities and groups of the past?

- Jim Jones and the Jonestown cult from the San Francisco Bay Area in the 1970s. To his followers, Jones was a messiah with all the answers to life and death.[14]
- Bhagwan Shree Rajneesh of the 1980s, who taught a version of self-enlightenment and the fluidity of the soul.[15]
- Judy "JZ" Zebra Knight, the female medium supposedly channeling a spiritual entity Ramtha to guide the decisions and lives of followers.[16]
- The Branch Davidians, led by David Koresh of the 1990s. Koresh was to be the final prophet and the messiah to his followers.[17]

Teachers from previous decades recall the discussions in classrooms about the latest *truths* that had come along with the personalities claiming to have divine revelation. Other groups, such as the Church of Scientology, mind and religious sciences, and other American religious groups, that claim they are in touch with a *progressive* Almighty are still converting people to their beliefs and causes.

Teachers and parents need to understand the impacts these have upon society. There are lasting effects of secular views that have deposited wares in the lives of their students and children. People must understand that current efforts to convert students and change American culture are steeped in ambition to stimulate conversion to progressive beliefs on sexuality, gender, marriage, religion, and politics as well as enlisting an army to the movement to declassify biological identity. Change is always from one thing to another thing.

The strategy is clear. Culture changers use the courts. Entertainment icons and cultural elites utilize the avenues of social media as their strategy. Educators use curriculum to gain the confidences of a generation seeking to find itself. Forces are aligned to shift American schools into complete social agencies and, in the process, reduce the focus on academics.

The Cult of the Individual

Education over the years has been considered as somewhat messianic.[18] Educational fads are cultlike, focusing on the enlightenment of the individual while holding to an *exclusive oneness* in belief and practice that all can choose to experience. Also cultlike is the fluidity that is expected as one advances through stages and levels of awareness as each person marches through a program focusing on spiritual, social, or emotional outcomes.

Fads, like cults, also have spokespersons, or leaders, who step forward to become examples of the newest and best versions of self. This is the classical sense of toxic cults dating back some fifty years. The more modern version is that the individual has had an emotional awakening.

It is in this sense, that twenty-first-century education is evolving and has many of the earmarks of a new type of cult. Rather than become a disciple of a guru or a mystic leader, *the woke folk*[19] are in touch with their own personal and social awareness. This includes their own personalized claim of self-divinity. Self-worship has become their ultimate expression of sacrifice on the altar of emotional identity and feelings.

Regardless of the group or the leader, whether religious or secular, there are two overarching commonalities. First, there is the identity of oneself, discovered through some life event. The second is that the leaders believe and feel that the teachings are the newest and most accurate truth on a subject to date.

From Shirley McClain's 1983 statement of *I am god*, to the current *I am god and my choices are my self-worship*, the seat of personal authority has not changed all that much. In a rights-driven society, Americans tend to think each is master of one's own destiny. The concerning part of this rests squarely in the notion of *I am in charge*. Schools are hefty social agencies and have so many social issues they take on daily that academics are often sacrificed for building students' social and emotional skills. Again, the messianic moniker applies here.

As the theologian B. B. Warfield wrote, "He who begins by seeking God within himself may end up confusing himself with God."[20] Being one's own god brings with it huge responsibilities. Being human brings with it huge accountabilities. With accountabilities come consequences. But here is where schools step in *to save* and to minimize accountabilities and responsibilities in favor of social justice and restorative justice.

Relevance to Schools

Not all teachers have the same views of culture and society. However, as the teaching corps, as well as parents, finds itself younger and more progressive, there is a greater opportunity for society to be shifted further and further away from traditions of the past.

Where does education fit in this mix of cults and fads? This is a relevant question. From Dewey to Gates to Darling-Hammond, beliefs about education over the years have been adopted and placed into practice. Time brings changes. One has to look no further than to recent history with George W. Bush's academic high-stakes pressure with No Child Left Behind legislation, which required 100 percent of all students to be academically *proficient* by the year 2014. Directly afterward, the Obama administration's national academic Race to the Top and Common Core, along with the push for national standards and talks of national curriculum controversies,[21] captured the attention of all educators. Each was relevant in its historical context yet now deemed faddish in looking back.

But where is the nation now? Where are our public schools in relation to the fatiguing focus on academic assessments of the past couple of decades? *First*, many public schools have adopted social-emotional learning and are spending significant in-class instructional time on social and emotional issues, including teaching students how to navigate their own emotions with today's cultural and moral paradigm shifts.

Some teachers proclaim they teach love, tolerance, and openness. Yet, when someone espouses beliefs that stand against the trends of current culture, he or she is suddenly unlovely, intolerable, and closed-minded. This is problematic because the very values that are to accompany an exclusive set of teachings or faddish programs turn out to be one-sided. As a result, moving away from academics, as such, is a likely response to the fads of the past, many of which would be likely to generate additional emotional toxicity over time.

Second, when it comes to political discussions that arise in classrooms, if a student's comments fit an acceptable narrative, they are extolled. Students with opposing viewpoints may otherwise be marginalized as uninformed or intolerant. Their parents, if they espouse similar viewpoints, would be labeled as ignorant, uneducated, unenlightened, or even deplorable.

Teachers who do not validate all sides of the disagreements demonstrate their lack of objectivity. These are not the marks of openness and choice. Without an academic allowance of debate, toxic and harmful classrooms are established and become points of departure for heated dissent.

Education Culture Has Changed

There is no secret that the United States is headlong into one of its most concerning teacher shortages in recent history. This shortage comes at a time when public school enrollments are swelling. Multiple researchers affirm that American school culture is partly the cause for some of the reasons leading to current teacher attrition. They found that overall school culture and the working environment have taken their tolls on teachers.

Parents have steadily been removing their children from public schools and, those who can afford it, have placed students in private schools. The United States has seen steady but slightly increasing enrollments in private K–12 schools (estimated six million), with numbers of students in those schools averaging between 250 and 500 students.[22]

Public charter schools enroll another 3.1 million students.[23] Homeschools serve another estimated 2.5 million students, and exclusive or blended K–12 online school coursework is estimated at nearly three million annually.[24] This means that, although some fifty-one million students will attend public schools in 2019–2020, another fifteen million students will not be attending traditional public schools by choice.[25]

American education is being affected by legislation in a number of ways. States have opened the door to school choice, which has added another educational dimension into the K–12 mix. The bottom line is that an increasing number of parents are enrolling their children in alternatives to public schools, as they determine what is best for their children. This means one out of four do not attend traditional public schools. Some of these actions have disquieted the status quo. This change in American education culture brings the issue in another direction: the toxic environment faced by teachers every day.

Any discussion that connects toxicity and culture brings with it certain assumptions and implications. The assumptions may at first glance yield a default concerning drug abuse among students in America's schools. That would be a fair assumption. Certainly, drugs are an American school problem and a scourge upon the nation and should be placed in the sphere of classical discourse on toxicity in American culture. However, there are also other factors that are prominent in elevating toxicity in American schools and must also be addressed.

Although the term *toxic* is tossed about these days as an all-purpose term, the basic idea behind toxicity is the impression of an element of something with at least adverse negative effects or, at most, something deadly. Poisoning includes the body but also includes poisoning of the soul, the mind, and the emotions. Each of these is as important as the others. Accordingly, the nation's schools and teachers need to avoid escalating toxicity by what they teach and how they teach it.

Resegregation

After the progress made over the past fifty years on social and racial issues, America's communities are experiencing a resurgence of re-segregation along racial, ethnic, religious, and sexual and gender lines. Squarely in the center of this resurgence of re-segregation are America's schools and communities at large, which also began to evidence signs of segregation through self-marginalization.

Many of America's cities are polarized by demographics, which leaves schools directly in the crosshairs of this polarization. However, since teachers are more gregarious about their beliefs and are moving toward more conscious expressions of their personal beliefs in shaping the ways they teach, the fundamental aspects of civic participation are changing.

Some teachers have become activists for one or more causes, unabashed to share their beliefs with their students, regardless of the ages of their students. While this activity attracts some to teaching, a number of teachers are leaving because they believe the practice of teacher activism detracts from teaching and slants student learning.[26]

When social agency becomes as important as academic urgency, students run the risk of becoming civic activists, in line with the social causes determined as just by secular groups pressing forward with the idea of segregation. Certainly, this issue is not front and center in the minds of most elementary and middle schoolers or in the minds of most of their teachers. Forcing it to be as such only created additional toxicity to an environment for teachers who just want to do their jobs and teach.[27] Yet there are activists calling for a separation of Americans based on what had already been constitutionally decided. However, this time, the segregation is being called for by choice.[28]

In the past, there was also a greater tendency for teachers of older students to tackle more sensitive or controversial issues in schools. Such sensitive issues were often left untouched in lower grades among younger students. This is no longer the case.[29] There are teacher-activists at all levels teaching ideas about sex and gender and contravening parents' rearing on marriage and relationships and blurring moral lines that had once been clearly drawn in schools.[30]

Violence and Killing

America is toxic because it tolerates and even promotes violence and death cultures. Every time there is a mass shooting there is a call by some politicians to make sweeping changes to laws, with the assumption that laws can end violence and killing in the United States. There are cases to be made on several sides of the debate over guns and violence in this nation. Nevertheless, there is no mistaking that America's children—while at home and at school—are exposed regularly to traumas that result in psychological, physical, or emotional harm.

Presidents have been blamed for everything from being the cause of our nation's Civil War, to creating the incitement for mass murderers in our nation's history. Regardless of the politics involved, violence and killing will always be a part of open society in an established death culture. Despite efforts to make the world a safer place, violence and killing are a part of every culture, and the United States is no exception.[31]

As horrific as mass murders are, the causes for such crimes are many. Placing the blame on any one aspect of culture is to miss the mark. The effects that an open culture have on those with everything from mental illness, to drug addiction, to those bullied and ostracized are real. The culture of violence and death for a majority of Americans also includes the abortion industry. Inner-city murders are seldom reported, and an education system that has stripped all moral teachings for a feelings-based search for truth only adds to the toxic nature of America's culture of death. Diminishing life's value at any level increases toxicity. Daily exposure to toxic beliefs is essentially violence upon the moral and spiritual realities of students. This is the kind of violence that goes beyond the body and affects the soul. There is little wonder why so many millennial adults and Gen Z students feel a sense of despair and hopelessness.

Hopelessness Is Toxic

A decline in moral clarity is often a precursor to gradual slippage in moral purpose. When children are involved, moral clarity can become moral confusion very quickly. One of the by-products of this decline and slippage is a sense of hopelessness. Teachers speak of student hopelessness enjoined with its cousin *apathy*.

Hopelessness sometimes leads students to lash out in anger and violence. Sometimes, this destruction is personal. Other times, it is directed toward objects as well as others. Although some would blame a certain level of violence on a problem associated with masculinity, the reality is that a culture with confused moral moorings provides little hope for students. American culture seems to be competing with itself by both promoting and countering toxicity by taking sides. Such a practice negates the very things it affirms. Teachers are on the forefront of this dilemma.

So what causes violence and killing? The easy answer is people. Beyond that response, there are far too many complexities. No one would argue that violence is not toxic. Likewise, most argue that toxicity is not the sole cause of the violence. Even if violence could perfectly be linked to one or more causes, the debate would still rage onward. Olivia Goldhill exemplifies the crux of the debate: "There is no credible way of predicting whether someone is capable of committing murder: science has not revealed any tell-tale signs that a seemingly normal person is on the path to violent criminality."[32]

Correlation Is Not Prediction

One researcher may argue that it is not possible to predict a person's acts of violence, even if in the past he or she acted violently. Another researcher might argue that studying historical acts of violence always traces back to inputs that are toxic. The reality that is ignored is that an accumulation of influences is probably the cause of the cause.

Violence is an act, and a truly toxic act. In most cases toxic acts arise from toxic inputs. However, violence is not just a physical act. Where the breaking point is for many who act out violently is unclear. In America today, the greater the number of toxic inputs, the greater the chance of something violent occurring as a result.

The continuous bombardment of negative inputs that Americans experience have far too many people near the edge between tolerance and patience and subsequent actions of intolerance and impatience. Children are demonstrating more adultlike behaviors and carry with them more anger than they should. Some of these displays are prompted because of traumas they faced sometimes in their lives. Below are six examples of negative cultural inputs that have been alleged to have caused violence.

- Politicians' regular use of the media to criticize or marginalize one or more groups[33]
- Radical groups that use social media to promote violence against law enforcement and to cause civil unrest[34]
- Violence in athletics that leads to head injuries, which may prompt domestic violence[35]
- Drug and alcohol abuse at parties, which may lead to sexual violence and crimes committed[36]
- Hate language and hate groups that are left to grow on the Internet, which may lead followers to commit acts of violence[37]
- Violent video games and players mimicking violence in reality[38]

Robert Burton, former associate director of the Department of Neuroscience at the University of California, San Francisco Medical Center at Mount Zion, examined thirty years of research data, including several recent meta-analyses. He established that (1) psychiatrists and psychologists are twice as likely to be wrong about predicting violence as they are to predict it might occur, (2) there is no valid scientific instrument, to date, that can determine who will and who will not commit violence, and (3) the *theories of mind* should be rethought and based on evidence.[39]

Burton concludes, "All good theories are predictive. Sooner or later, they need supporting evidence. If experts cannot tell us who will be violent, or commit suicide, or is lying, isn't it time for us to reconsider there are real and practical limits to our belief in Theories of Mind (ToM)?" Does this mean schools can comfortably ignore any negative cognitive or emotional that affects students?

Concerns about Toxic Inputs

As a nation, America should be concerned about the inputs of information that students process in our classrooms. Teachers are influencers and are called this for a reason. Teachers provide some of the greatest influences in the lives of students.

This raises an appropriate question:

If we're incapable of knowing what others are capable of, do we know what we could potentially do? Most of us, after all, have thought about committing murder. David Buss, professor of psychology at the University of Texas-Austin, surveyed 5,000 people for his book *The Murderer Next Door: Why the Mind Is Designed to Kill* and found that 91% of men and 84% of women had thought about killing someone, often with very specific hypothetical victims and methods in mind.[40]

Triggers and Drivers
Douglas Fields adds that people are biologically predisposed, like animals, to violence in given situations. Even good people can go bad and commit horrible actions.[41] These conclusions should be enough to cause serious concern about the amount of toxicity and the toxic triggers building within an already fragile, emotionally charged generation of children and young adults. In a perfect world, people would be able to recognize every sign and every affect that has the potential to disable a young mind and heart. In such a world, people would also understand the traits of triggers that lead to some sort of response, whether violent or not.

A trigger *sets off* something, and far too often the things that are manifest emerge from an emotional reaction to a word committed against them. The fact is that life's circumstances are toxic enough. *Teachers should not be the catalysts of toxicity.*[42]

If an understanding of negative inputs could be ascertained for each person, then people could "understand that the jolt of rage . . . when . . . late for an important meeting and someone cuts through traffic is a misfiring, rather than an appropriate response."[43] Yet there is no escaping the fact that "societal pressures, including cultural norms and legal guidelines, do influence our biological impulses to murder, and the rate of human violence varies considerably across time periods and cultures."[44]

Teenage students "should be taught about the biological triggers for aggression . . . [even though] the prefrontal cortex—the threat detection mechanism—is not fully developed in teenagers."[45] Teaching self-control is a good start. However, it is no longer culturally appropriate to hold some students accountable for their words and behaviors. This sends a negative input to students who are not part of the favored cultural group.

What causes students to snap violently and what are their triggers?[46] As First Corinthians declares, *For who among men knows the thoughts of a man except the spirit of the man which is in him?*[47]

Confusion in cultural messaging is a seed of many frustrations in America's schools. If teachers and schools focused more on academics and less on socially and emotionally triggering inputs our students would benefit greatly. For example, Americans believe they have freedom of speech yet are unwilling to hear words that are contrary to their beliefs. Disagreements such as these sometimes lead to verbal confrontations and even violence. Another example is the Second Amendment.

There are some who would use the Second Amendment right properly and others who would abuse it in harming or committing crimes against others. Is the answer less freedom, as the nation deals with toxic topics and expressions of rights that might cause harm? Or is the answer adding more toxicity to combat an already established toxic environment? As a nation, America needs to continue to work out these seemingly conflicting questions, and the answers are not as easy as politicians suggest.

The Media
What qualifies as media in American culture? Any avenue or conduit whereby people find information can be defined as media. There is news media, arts and entertainment media, information media, sports media, and social media. A regular diet of any of these media can easily produce hefty doses of negativity and a bounty of heated discussions.

In terms of drivers of culture, there are numerous accounts of younger athletes emulating their favorite sports stars. Coarse language has become more acceptable in culture because a steady diet of its use bombards the ears of children and adults. Words deemed vulgar to one generation are now widely used in verbal and adjectival forms. There is no debate over whether what we see and hear as Americans affects our behaviors. The only questions are *how much* and *how often?*

News analysts and cable television personalities seem to have less regard for balanced journalism. Dating back to the Clinton administration, cable news networks began to evidence less objectivity and more advocacy journalism. During the administration of George W. Bush and carrying into the Obama and Trump administrations, toxic news coverage became more of a partisan staple.

Social media platforms have done deep dives toward partisanship. With the news of Google and the efforts it undertook to thwart the campaign and election of Trump as president, media outlets, including online news groups, have been too politically slanted and biased. Many on-air personalities are now activists and critics, always competing for ratings.

Opinions are dished out and shaped by the media for the American information consumer. Add to this shaping the Internet and the constant barrage of immediate postings of the latest headlines, whether real or contrived, and masses of people are infected with slanted and slick information.

There is no doubt that an ever-increasing percentage of news coverage is meant to inflame, incite, and take sides. Each entity tries to best its competition by posting the first and foremost authoritative set of characters and images. All of this is meant to serve emotions over cognition and to convince consumers to buy the objective of a particular perspective. In terms of the Internet, the number of likes and savvy website optimizers make certain to both hold and inform readers.

The election of Donald Trump as president demonstrated the height of toxicity quite clearly. For example, a few media outlets had a clear pro-Trump bias, while many others had just the opposite. Within weeks of Trump's election, the practice of labeling the president and those who voted for him as racists began.

This type of toxicity does little for open dialogue. In fact, just the opposite occurs. Violence against people wearing Trump attire began to pop up nationally. There is little doubt that President Trump has added to this labeling and increase of violence by his own toxic remarks, both by the media and online. The contrast of media serving up toxic truths and the clarion call to avoid certain stations because of fake new does little to settle the toxicity that often rears its ugly head in America's schoolrooms.

Religion
There is no avoiding the fact that America was founded on Judeo-Christian principles and European political philosophies and that religious freedom was a hallmark of many of the first colonies. Christianity, in particular, was the foundation of much of our legal system, imported by European settlers. There is a trend by progressive historians to revise American history and establish the idea that America has always been a systemically racist nation.

This trend has stoked fears on behalf of people expressing pride in their nation and its accomplishments and advances. In fact, there are people unwilling to fly the American flag in some communities for fear of being labeled as racist oppressors or nationalists merely because they are proud of Old Glory. Some who see the flag are triggered and offended because of the revisionism of American history and the offenses they have been made aware of by newly established American history curriculum.

From its inception, America has placed a premium on the freedom of religion. States were eventually formed to enable people to practice as they saw fit or not to practice religion at all. Especially during the periods immediately following the American Revolution, the Articles of Confederation and the Constitution were developed to demonstrate the importance of our history as well as to allow religious freedom.

It remains clear that the guarantee of religious freedom in both belief and practice is established by the First Amendment to the Constitution. These guarantees, along with restrictions placed on Congress not to infringe, remain important to this day in terms of traditional historians versus progressive historical revisionism.

The Supreme Court of the United States has weighed in on these matters. The Court's decisions play a direct role in cultural change around freedom of religion. Some of these changes prompt heated debate to this day. Thus, some of the United States' landmark religion cases that have caused more than their share of toxicity over the years include:[48]

- *Reynolds v. United States* (1879): Federal law banning polygamy is upheld.
- *Cantwell v. Connecticut* (1940): The state cannot determine which is and which is not religious truth and infringe on peaceful expressions of beliefs.
- *Everson v. Board of Education* (1947): It is constitutional for students who attend private schools to have their parents reimbursed for bus transportation costs, regardless of religion.
- *Braunfield v. Brown* (1961): Blue laws, which allowed only certain types of stores to remain open on Sundays, have secular bases and did not make any religious practices unlawful.
- *Torcaso v. Watkins* (1961): A requirement for a political candidate to state a belief in God violated the Establishment Clause of the First Amendment.
- *Engel v. Vitale* (1962): School-led prayer deemed unconstitutional.
- *Sherbert v. Werner* (1963): The denial of unemployment benefits because a person turned down a job that required work on the Sabbath impeded the Free Exercise Clause of the First Amendment.
- *School District of Abington Township, Pennsylvania, v. Schempp* (1963): Compulsory daily Bible reading violated both the Establishment Clause and the Free Exercise Clause of the First Amendment.
- *Murray v. Curlett* (1963): Revisited *Abington v. Schempp* in Maryland and found that compulsory Bible reading and recitation of the Lord's Prayer violated both the Establishment Clause and the Free Exercise Clause of the First Amendment.

- *Epperson v. Arkansas* (1968): Arkansas law prohibiting the teaching of evolution violated the First Amendment. The First Amendment does not permit a state to require teaching and learning to be tailored to the principle or prohibitions of any religious sect or dogma.
- *Lemon v. Kurtzman* (1971): Three-pronged test established to determine how a religious school can use state funds.
- *Wisconsin v. Yoder* (1972): Amish adolescents could be exempt from state law requiring school attendance for all 14- to 16-year-olds.
- *McDaniel v. Paty* (1978): People serving as clergy can also run for and hold public office.
- *Stone v. Graham* (1980): State legislatures that mandate public posting of the Ten Commandments violate the Establishment Clause of the First Amendment.
- *Mueller v. Allen* (1982): Parents were allowed to deduct state income tax expenses for schooling of their children, including those who attended private schools. As with the three-pronged Lemon Test, there was no excessive entanglement of the state with religion.
- *Marsh v. Chambers* (1983): Invoking divine guidance on a body of legislators, by means of an opening prayer is not establishment of any religion, but a tolerable acknowledgment of widely held beliefs of many Americans.
- *Lynch v. Donnelly* (1984): Nativity scenes are celebrations and depictions of a national holiday and not a violation of the Establishment Clause of the First Amendment.
- *Wallace v. Jaffree* (1985): A law authorizing a silent prayer of meditation period violated the Establishment Clause of the First Amendment.
- *Edwards v. Aguillard* (1987): A law requiring the teaching of creationism if evolution is taught in schools is deemed unconstitutional because it failed the three-prongs of the Lemon Test.
- *County of Allegheny v. ACLU* (1989): Including a menorah with a Christmas tree, along with a sign that saluted liberty, conveyed a message of freedom of belief and did not violate the Establishment Clause of the First Amendment.
- *Board of Education of Westside Community Schools v. Mergens* (1990): The Equal Access Act of 1990 allows students of a religious group to meet on school campuses, with the same rights held by secular groups.
- *Lee v. Weisman* (1992): Clergy-led prayer at a public school graduation ceremony violated the Establishment Clause of the First Amendment.

- *Santa Fe Independent School District v. Doe* (2000): Student-initiated prayers at football games violate the Establishment Clause of the First Amendment.
- *Elk Grove Unified School District v. Newdow* (2004): The phrase "under God," in the flag salute cannot possibly lead to the establishment of a religion.

Over the years, religion has been one of a hotbed of many toxic cultural upheavals that eventually affected students and schools. Depending on the political and philosophical makeup of the Court, decisions sometimes intensify cultural divides. For example, cases such as *The State of Tennessee v. John Thomas Scopes* (1925), *Roe v. Wade* (1973), *Obergefell v. Hodges* (2015), and *Trump v. Hawaii* (2018) touch nerves on all sides of issues ranging from evolution to abortion, to same-sex couple benefits and marriage to travel bans to nations designated as hotbeds for terrorists.

Changing laws changes culture. Often, changes in culture will upset some groups viewing the actions of the Court as wrong and its decisions as toxic. Some issues will never be mediated, and there will never be a common ground for the majority. The reason is that, given current political and moral climates in the United States, a moderate view on some issues is not possible.

The general conclusion is that these cases, and other cases such as these, demonstrate at least six areas of continued toxic cultural conflicts between religion and secular culture: (1) church and state, (2) religion and science, (3) religion in the public square and public discourse, (4) religion and the workplace, (5) religion and ethics, and health care and abortion, and (6) religion in the matters of marriage and family definitions.[49]

September 11, 2001, Changed Culture

Despite the statement of George W. Bush that Islam was a religion of peace and that there was no war against Islam, the facts did not line up across much of the American populace. Americans generally were skeptical of the separation of the Islamic religion from actions of jihadist violence. Adding to this skepticism were Muslim leaders who were not willing to come out publicly and denounce the terrorist acts.

Islamophobia
Since 9-11-01, millions of Muslims now live in America and hold political office, and these American Muslims have been busy building their communities.[50]

Nearly an entire generation has no recollection of the 2001 tragedy and does not possess the same emotional connection to the event.

Even so, today, there is still a fear of Islam,[51] as Americans are seeing more and more Muslims move to the United States and mosques being erected in their once Christian neighborhoods.[52] Blocks long of men on their knees praying in public, as communities are treated to the call to prayer over mosque speakers, is something no one would have envisioned after 9-11.[53]

As a sign of progress, the increase of Muslim immigration under the Obama administration helped many Americans to understand not only the religion better but the Muslim culture as well.[54] However, recent elections of Muslims on local, state, and national levels have caused stirs as some outspoken Muslims are expressing anti-Semitic views.[55]

Islam has become toxic in some communities because of the insistence of groups pressuring local governments to recognize and acquiesce to the sovereignty of Muslim culture and lifestyle. For example, some growing Muslim communities are demanding that pork products be banned from school lunches.[56] Others are speaking out against the styles of clothing being worn. Still others are speaking out against certain curricula that teaches values contrary to Muslim values.

In response, which also adds to this community toxicity, Jews and Christians are also speaking out about the increases of anti-Semitism and anti-Christian actions in their communities. The desire to maintain faith and culture, rather than to assimilate, brings with it a spirit of distinction that is sometimes in conflict with established community standards. Can there possibly be a middle ground?

Anti-Christian Bias in the Media

Some in the media have taken to labeling Christians as racists—for expressing disagreement with Islamic teaching and practice—even when race has nothing to do with the issue at hand. When a Muslim adherent argues that the Quran is against homosexuality or that a wife may be struck by her husband for the sake of discipline, few in the media call out these beliefs and practices as homophobic or misogynistic. However, when a Christian uses the Bible for what has also been part of his or her teaching in the faith on homosexuality or traditional marriage, the outcome is generally different.

Christophobia

There is a twenty-first-century Christophobia in American culture. Americans live at a time when groups of people have been given status as a race, when race has nothing to do with who they are. Such practices by any segment of the media are not only intolerant, they are incendiary and toxic. And this is probably the point: setting up conflict for the sake of headlines. As a result of these actions, it appears religion is now connected to race in terms of all-purpose denigration.

If some revisionist scholars have their way, Christianity would be purely a White man's religion forced upon subjugated peoples of the world as they were colonized and enslaved. Such teachings are meant to erode national unity—the kind of unity that some think is systemically racist, anyway. What will students come away with about America if much of what they hear is a progressive message advancing a racist Eurocentric narrative? It is up to the teacher to bring truth to students. Is it truth to saddle the children with the sins of a nation's past?

Added Confusion

Children are learning to use the term *racist* when a friend disagrees with him or her. Parents are quick to call racism on teachers when they hear students come home with what a teacher supposedly stated in class. Emotions are so volatile that students who wear clothing or hats trigger a person to angry actions.

One reason for today's confusing and challenging school environment is that twenty-first-century teachers come into the workplace with different fundamental ideologies and beliefs that stand in contrast to those of previous generations. Yet these generations must work side by side. Cultural clashes are often centered on traditional versus newly defined progressive values. For example, teachers in some communities proclaim that respect for life and family is held in contempt merely because it cuts against the grain of emotionally driven secular beliefs. There is no longer a Golden Rule practiced as such in schools. Culture has secularized the rule to focus more on the individual, as evidenced by the twist of *Do unto others before they do unto you.*

America has gone from describing issues for debate to the mention of similar issues as racist, hateful, and toxic. Teachers at all levels are finding this to be true when classroom disagreements occur on topics such as religion, politics, marriage, family, and gender.

Sometimes, conflicts become so heated that people who merely perceive a look, comment, joke, or gesture conclude that any one of these expressions is justification of unsafe feelings or micro-aggressions. Another aspect is the inconsistency of the cultural faddishness of the direction of feelings. For example, a person who feels like he or she is of another race or desires this feeling to be recognized by others is both chastised and supported on social media. On the one hand, such a person is celebrated for his or her chosen identity but dismissed by others for appropriating something of another group's biological identity. Confusion is not clarity.

I Feel, Therefore I Am

In terms of one of the classical and historical American institutions, it seems that the Christian church has let down its members by not focusing on biblical and traditional definitions of things that mattered so much to this nation's development—things like marriage and morality. The lukewarm theology has produced several by-products, one of which is the focus on love and feelings. This is evidenced by much of the worship and imbalanced teachings on the love of God and acceptance of anything and everything in the name of this love, including hedonism and self-pleasures.

While it may not be toxic for an *adult* to claim an identity not assigned at birth, the issue becomes very toxic when involving *children* making the same choices. Add to this legislation that forces people to recognize and acknowledge the claim of another and the toxicity escalates.

Twenty-first-century schools are full of students who are determining their identity by their feelings. This, then, is the essence of the modern identity movement: "I feel, therefore I am." Hence, this is one of the newer traits that has emerged from a fundamentally volatile toxic society.

Notes

1. Harvey Mansfield. "Parties vs. factions in America." Hoover Institution. September 21, 2017. Retrieved from https://www.hoover.org/research/parties-vs-factions-america.

2. Paul Negri and Kathy Casey (eds). John Stuart Mill. *On Liberty*. 2002. Minneola, New York: Dover Thrift Publications.

3. David L. Holmes. "The Founding Fathers, Deism, and Christianity." *Encyclopedia Britannica*. December 21, 2006. Retrieved from https://www.britannica.com/topic/The-Founding-Fathers-Deism-and-Christianity-1272214. Cf. Bill Flax. "Was America founded as a Christian nation?" *Forbes*. September 25, 2012. Retrieved from https://www.forbes.com/sites/billflax/2012/09/25/was-america-founded-as-a-christian-nation/#4f125aed4e7b.

4. Peter Schuck. "Against (and for) Madison: An essay in praise of factions." *Yale Law and Policy Review*. 1996. 15(2): 553–597. Retrieved from https://pdfs.semanticscholar.org/2e9f/71ca3e82ea9c0a1b7459524640f2dbb8c191.pdf.

5. James Madison. "The Federalist No. 10: The utility of the union as a safeguard against domestic faction and insurrection." *Daily Advertiser*. November 22, 1787. Retrieved from https://www.constitution.org/fed/federa10.htm.
6. Ibid.
7. Ibid.
8. Ibid.
9. Ibid.
10. Ibid.
11. Ibid.
12. Ibid.
13. Ibid.
14. Lesley Kennedy. "Inside Jonestown: How Jim Jones trapped followers and forced suicides." *History Channel*. March 18, 2019. Retrieved from https://www.history.com/news/jonestown-jim-jones-mass-murder-suicide.
15. J. Gordon Melton. "Bhagwan Shree Rajneesh." *Encyclopedia Britannica*. No date. Retrieved from https://www.britannica.com/biography/Bhagwan-Shree-Rajneesh.
16. Judy Zebra Knight. "JZ Knight and Ramtha note 42 years of a remarkable collaboration this week." February 18, 2019. Retrieved from http://www.jzknight.com/.
17. Staff. "Biography: David Koresh." *PBS Frontline*. No date. Retrieved from https://www.pbs.org/wgbh/pages/frontline/waco/davidkoresh.html.
18. Rousas John Rushdoony. 1995 (1963). The messianic character of American education. Vallecito, California: Ross House Books.
19. "Woke." https://www.merriam-webster.com/words-at-play/woke-meaning-origin.
20. Benjamin Breckinridge Warfield. "Mysticism and Christianity." *The works of Benjamin B. Warfield*. 1991. Grand Rapids, Michigan: Baker Book House. Vol. 9, pp. 649–666.
21. Ernest J. Zarra III. *The wrong direction for today's schools: The impact of Common Core on American education*. 2015. Lanham, Maryland: Rowman & Littlefield Publishers. Cf. Nicholas Tampio. *Common Core: National education standards and the threat to democracy*. 2018. Baltimore, Maryland: Johns-Hopkins Press.
22. Staff. "Fast Facts: Back to school statistics 2019." National Center for Education Statistics. Retrieved from https://nces.ed.gov/fastfacts/display.asp?id=372. Cf. Staff. "Private school statistics at a glance." *Council for American Private Education*. Retrieved from https://www.capenet.org/facts.html.
23. Rebecca David and Kevin Hesla. "Estimated public charter school enrollment, 2017–2018." *Public Charters*. March 2018. Retrieved from https://www.publiccharters.org/sites/default/files/documents/2018-03/FINAL%20Estimated%20Public%20Charter%20School%20Enrollment%2C%202017-18.pdf.
24. Brian D. Ray. "Research facts on homeschooling." *National Home Education Research Institute*. January 7, 2019. Retrieved from https://www.nheri.org/research-facts-on-homeschooling/.

25. Staff. "Infographic: Growth of K–12 digital learning." *Connections Academy*. Retrieved from https://www.connectionsacademy.com/news/growth-of-k-12-online-education-infographic.

26. Tricia Niesz. "When teachers become activists." *Phi Delta Kappan*. May 24, 2018. Retrieved from https://www.kappanonline.org/niesz-teacher-activist-groups/.

27. Ibid.

28. Jemele Hill. "It's time for Black athletes to leave White colleges." *Atlantic*. October 2019. Retrieved from https://www.theatlantic.com/magazine/archive/2019/10/black-athletes-should-leave-white-colleges/596629/.

29. Molly Pulda. "More students are becoming activists. Teachers can help strengthen their voice." *EdSurge*. January 21, 2019. Retrieved from https://www.edsurge.com/news/2019-01-21-more-students-are-becoming-activists-teachers-can-help-strengthen-their-voice.

30. Jennifer Gonzalez. "How ordinary teachers become activists." *Cult of Pedagogy*. May 10, 2015. Retrieved from https://www.cultofpedagogy.com/teacher-activism-education-reform/. Cf. Michael Brown. "An activist educator says that teaching is political." *American Family Association*. July 24, 2019. Retrieved from https://www.afa.net/the-stand/culture/2019/07/an-activist-educator-says-that-teaching-is-political/.

31. Rachel Kleinfeld. "Why are some societies so violent, and can they be made safe?" *Carnegie Endowment for International Peace*. Retrieved from https://carnegieendowment.org/2018/11/19/why-are-some-societies-so-violent-and-can-they-be-made-safe-pub-77749.

32. Olivia Goldhill. "A neuroscientist who studies rage says we're all capable of doing something terrible." *Quartz*. August 4, 2018. Retrieved from https://qz.com/1348203/a-neuroscientist-who-studies-rage-says-were-all-capable-of-doing-something-terrible/.

33. Victor Pickard. "Media and politics in the age of Trump." *Origins*. Ohio State University and Miami University History Departments. Vol. 10. Issue 2. November 2016. Retrieved from https://origins.osu.edu/article/media-and-politics-age-trump.

34. Staff. "ANTIFA should have to play by the same rules as everyone else on social media. Suspend now." *Change.org*. 2019. Retrieved from https://www.change.org/p/silicon-valley-antifa-should-have-to-play-by-the-same-rules-as-everyone-else-on-social-media-suspend-now.

35. L. Turkstra, D. Jones, and Hon. L. Toler. "Brain injury and violent crime." *Brain Injury*. 2009. 17(1): 39–47. Retrieved from https://www.tandfonline.com/doi/abs/10.1080/02699050210000101 22.

36. Staff. "Understanding the connection between drug addiction, alcoholism, and violence." *American Addiction Centers*. August 21, 2019. Retrieved from https://americanaddictioncenters.org/rehab-guide/addiction-and-violence.

37. Liam Stack. "Over 1,000 hate groups are now active in United States, civil rights group says." *New York Times*. February 20, 2019. Retrieved from. https://www.nytimes.com/2019/02/20/us/hate-groups-rise.html. Cf. Staff. "How do violent ex-

tremists make contact?" *Federal Bureau of Investigation*. 2019. Retrieved from https://www.fbi.gov/cve508/teen-website/how.

38. Craig A. Anderson. "Violent video games: Myths, facts, and unanswered questions." *American Psychological Association*. October 2003. Retrieved from https://www.apa.org/science/about/psa/2003/10/anderson. Cf. Art Markman. "The evidence that video games lead to violence is weak." *Psychology Today*. August 4, 2019. Retrieved from https://www.psychologytoday.com/us/blog/ulterior-motives/201908/the-evidence-video-games-lead-violence-is-weak.

39. Robert A. Burton. "The theory of mind myth." *Aeon*. July 23, 2018. Retrieved from https://aeon.co/essays/think-you-can-tell-what-others-are-thinking-think-again.

40. David Buss. *The murderer next door: Why the mind is designed to kill*. 2005. New York: Penguin Press. Cf. Olivia Goldhill. "A neuroscientist who studies rage says we're all capable of doing something terrible." *Quartz*. August 4, 2018. Retrieved from https://qz.com/1348203/a-neuroscientist-who-studies-rage-says-were-all-capable-of-doing-something-terrible/.

41. Douglas Fields. *Why we snap: Understanding the rage circuit in your brain*. 2015. New York: Penguin Random House. See chapter 2.

42. Douglas Fields. *Why we snap: Understanding the rage circuit in your brain*. See chapter 3.

43. Olivia Goldhill. "A neuroscientist who studies rage says we're all capable of doing something terrible." *Quartz*. August 4, 2018. Retrieved from https://qz.com/1348203/a-neuroscientist-who-studies-rage-says-were-all-capable-of-doing-something-terrible/.

44. Ibid.

45. Douglas Fields. *Why we snap: Understanding the rage circuit in your brain*. See chapter 2.

46. Douglas Fields. *Why we snap: Understanding the rage circuit in your brain*. See chapters 1, 3.

47. *The New American Standard Bible*, 1 Corinthians 2:11a.

48. Staff. "Religious liberty: Landmark Supreme Court cases." Bill of Rights Institute. 2019. Retrieved from https://billofrightsinstitute.org/cases/.

49. Joela Brown. "The struggle is real: Understanding the American 'culture war.'" Religion and Culture Forum. July 11, 2017. Retrieved from https://voices.uchicago.edu/religionculture/2017/07/11/the-struggle-is-real-understanding-the-american-culture-war-by-russell-d/. Cf. David French. "Two painful truths of America's religious culture war." *National Review*. September 9, 2019. Retrieved from https://www.nationalreview.com/2019/06/two-painful-truths-of-americas-religious-culture-war/.

50. Michael Jackman. "Everyone in Michigan should read this new report on the state's Muslims." *Detroit Metro Times*. September 14, 2017. Retrieved from https://www.metrotimes.com/news-hits/archives/2017/09/14/everyone-in-michigan-should-read-this-new-report-on-the-states-muslims.

51. Andrew Selsky. "Anti-sharia rallies this weekend worry Muslim leaders." *PBS News Hour*. June 9, 2017. Retrieved from https://www.pbs.org/newshour/nation/anti-sharia-rallies-this-weekend-worry-muslim-leaders.

52. Tanvi Misra. "Mosque NIMBYism: The neighborhood Muslim ban." *City Lab*. April 5, 2017. Retrieved from https://www.citylab.com/equity/2017/04/a-short-history-of-zoning-obstructionism-against-mosques/521829/.

53. John Leland. "Tension in a Michigan city over Muslims' call to prayer." *New York Times*. May 5, 2004. Retrieved from https://www.nytimes.com/2004/05/05/us/tension-in-a-michigan-city-over-muslims-call-to-prayer.html.

54. Naveed Jamali. "Why the US doesn't have a Muslim problem, and Europe does." *Foreign Policy Research Institute*. April 3, 2016. Retrieved from https://www.fpri.org/2016/04/us-doesnt-muslim-problem-europe/.

55. Susan Cornwell. "Democratic leaders back Muslim lawmaker after holocaust comments." *Reuters*. May 13, 2019. Retrieved from https://www.reuters.com/article/us-usa-congress-holocaust/u-s-democratic-leaders-back-muslim-lawmaker-after-holocaust-comments-idUSKCN1SJ2H8.

56. Teresa Welsh. "School must provide non-pork lunches for Jewish and Muslim students, court rules." *Miami Herald*. August 29, 2017. Retrieved from https://www.miamiherald.com/news/nation-world/world/article170135262.html.

CHAPTER TWO

~

Neo-Toxic Culture

Delusional gems, designed to flatten the playing field of human existence, keep on coming: Gender differences do not exist; you can change your sex just by saying so. Most men are savage rapists-in-waiting. There is no "debate" on climate change: the result funded by industry grants, has already been decided. White people should all be ashamed of themselves for having been born with the "wrong" skin. There is no such thing as a nation state. Borders are no longer necessary. Questioning immigration makes you a Nazi. Expressing what you think can ship you to prison.[1]

Along with the inheritance of some of America's toxic history, new additions are being linked with this legacy. Every day, students are exposed to beliefs, practices, and educational policies—many of which have less to do with academic achievement and much to do with social engineering. This exposure turns out to be in high contrast to the values of many students and their upbringing.

The time has come to defuse and detox many American public schools of their incendiary toxicity. Through professional development and practical tools, there is an excellent chance for education rehabilitation and for teachers to rise up and call for a return to the fundamental mission of schools in America—to educate students academically. Furthermore, focusing on the academic over the social will provide the platform for an informed citizenry, able to converse and discuss critical issues. But without an academic underpinning, all that remains is emotion and opinion.[2]

Certainly, some toxic issues in our nation's past remain front and center in American culture, and Americans may still remain on one side of the issue or the other. Many of these are illustrated in chapter 1. Some people simply do not want to let go of the past. Nevertheless, some of the present direction must be kept in check. The reason for this is a neo-toxicity that is rushing toward being firmly embedded in twenty-first-century American culture.

The Presidential Election of 2016

The election of Donald Trump raised the level of toxicity in the public square. Public school students and college students were agitated, and some teachers and professors stoked the agitation. Trump's efforts continued to raise the societal temperature by stunting a progressive trend toward liberal policies on race, gender, the environment, energy, the military, illegal immigration, the economy, and law enforcement. Additionally, some of the Obama-era policies began to be undermined, and Trump's executive orders inflamed many politicians.

There was a distinct conflict of values and political direction between presidents Obama and Trump and a very real toxic environment developed between the supporters on both sides. One side was accused of undermining the election of a new president, and the other side was accused of colluding with Russians to deny Hillary Clinton the presidency in 2016.

After the election of Donald Trump as the forty-fifth president of the United States, there was observed a rise in white supremacy propaganda on college campuses. According to the Anti-Defamation League (ADL), high-profile cases on the campuses of Texas State University, the University of Virginia, Vanderbilt University, and Michigan State University revealed a different level of racial boldness not observed during the Obama administration.[3]

However, what was seen during the Obama years was a hostility toward law enforcement, coinciding with subsequent killings of young black men and several assassinations of some members of different states' police forces.[4] There has been some debate as to whether President Obama's policies laid the groundwork for the election of President Trump,[5] nearly a one-hundred-eighty degree shift in policies.[6]

In terms of the political and social extremism on college campuses, "During the 2017–2018 academic year . . . the Center on Extremism recorded 292 instances of white supremacist propaganda on campuses. That's a 77-percent increase from the 165 cases it documented in the 2016–17 academic year."[7] These examples existed primarily in the forms of "posters and fliers [and] white supremacists' propaganda . . . continues to accelerate, both on and off campus, online and on the ground."[8] Are these incidents residuals of the Obama-era policies, the election of Donald Trump, or both?

For example, there are anecdotes of teachers violating school policy and creating environments that many would consider toxic. These were coming from both extremes of the political spectrum. A former teacher, Georgia Clark, a secondary teacher from Texas, used Twitter to request "assistance from the president to deal with 'illegal students' and 'drug dealers,'"[9] which she claimed were taking over the school. Clark wrote,

> Mr. President, Fort Worth Independent School District is loaded with illegal students from Mexico. . . . Carter-Riverside High School has been taken over by them. Drug dealers are on our campus and nothing was done to them when the drug dogs found the evidence. . . . I do not know what to do. Anything you can do to remove the illegals from Fort Worth would be greatly appreciated.[10]

There is also evidence today that public school teachers are using contemporary issues to stir up students and introduce civic activism through emotion. Critics of these actions have taken to social media to request that certain proactive teachers deescalate some of their rhetoric. But that is easier said than done with supporters piling on to defend both sides.

Emotional Addicts
American culture is newly addicted to the emotions that are generated by today's social and political intoxicants. Moreover, influencers are quick to seize upon differences and augment them with marginalizing rhetoric. America can thank social media and online sites for fanning some of the flames of cultural disagreements and turning them into piles of smoldering embers.[11]

Rising from the embers is a group of new teachers from Gen Z. What they all seem to have in common, regardless their backgrounds, is that each comes with his or her own personal beliefs and opinions on a range of issues. Some of these opinions are cemented into their psyches. For example, college students emerging from Gen Z are more action oriented and radicalized toward social causes.[12]

America has changed, and the nation is more divided today along generations, races, religions, and economics. America is now more polarized and even more toxic. There seem to be no social or educational institutions left unaffected by this change. Not everyone has a progressive mind-set about change. Not everyone is a traditionalist. Those who resist changes are being labeled by all-purpose pejoratives, not the least of which is the term *racist*.

Neo-Toxic All-Purpose Pejoratives

The all-purpose term *racist* now comes to school every day on the minds of many, if not on their lips. Some teachers are quick to apply the term to circumstances they believe are part of a larger problem within American culture. The word is used as an ad hominem conclusion about people with mere disagreements or who have conservative ideas that liberals disdain. The word *racist* is the all-purpose word meant to shut down cognition, debate, objectivity, and dialogue. It is meant to marginalize. As a result, dissenting views on issues pertaining to people are established as deplorable and hateful.

There is a very significant lesson to be learned by watching politicians speak about whether they regret saying or doing something. It is as if they are afraid of looking weaker than others. Often, they just double down or spin things to make themselves appear like they actually were right to be wrong.

What is it about our culture that no longer enables us to take responsibility for wrongdoings, improper words, or when someone else is seriously injured by personal attack by words or actions? Children today are quick to blame others or even some arbitrary outside force for their bad choices and the results of these choices. Some adults are no better.

There are at least three reasons people do not claim their wrongdoings and express sorrow or regret in today's neo-toxic culture. These include (1) fear of the consequences if the truth is told, (2) the inability to accept personal responsibility, and (3) the attitude of unwillingness to admit wrongdoing.

Liar, Liar?

People have very little trouble lying today. Consequences for even government officials have been minimized, and legal double standards are acceptable in culture. Making up stories that place the wrongdoer in the best light is now commonplace, and the *use any means* to arrive at the ends desired is the neo-toxic standard.

Apologies are few and far between these days. In order to apologize, one has to understand he or she was wrong in what he or she said or did. Since few ever arrive at this point of honesty, apologies are equally as self-serving as the actions in question. The bottom line is, if a person can lie and not have to deal with the consequences, then he or she resorts to lying. The bottom line is there is little fear of consequences.

Blame Shifter?

If a person is unable to bring someone else into the mix of sharing blame, then most people will defend their actions as just. Even when confronted with video evidence of wrongdoing, people claim the video is doctored or it is fake. Shifting blame is a subjective ethic, and we see this across culture, particularly in schools, as well as in adults in the workplace.

The shaming of another provides cover for a person's actions, and the ethic of splitting consequences somehow makes a true guilty party less culpable in his or her mind. The old excuse he made me do it *or* look what you made me do is still in style but on steroids.

Adults have shown children that the admission of being wrong is weak and that being proud of any attempt that makes him or her shine among others is best. Unfortunately, our progressive culture sees to it that there is no need for regret. There is no need to apologize. In fact, making a person admit to wrongdoing may now be classified as bullying, profiling, or targeting.

If a person is always right, he or she is never wrong. If a person is offended by the actions of another, then the offended must be a snowflake, weak and easily hurt. People go on the attack, usually ad hominem, when they are accused of something. Always being right and never saying *I am sorry for what I did or said to you* is a character flaw. It is also narcissism and arrogance that is in the way of humility.

Twenty-First-Century Neo-Toxic Issues

As stated in chapter 1, public education has become a kind of denomination of its own, which makes schools as places of worship. There are clear sets of doctrinal tenets, with expectations that young attendees will come away espousing the same beliefs.

Unbelievers and dissenters are shamed, and often this shaming is accomplished by a tactful teacher making every effort to balance the direction of the cultural climate and direction toward which the class is being steered and those with whom he or she must contend. Those who do not ascribe to the teachings can be marginalized and *shamed* for not being part of the status quo in schools.

The new fashionable bullying is to make certain those who do not comply are to be instructed as to the reasons they are troubled by agreeing.[13] Public schools are every bit as evangelistic about core beliefs as any church institution in America.

America is a flipped society. It is flipped because individuals have become much more important than the whole. This is not to say that individuals have not had protections under law. However, *identity movements* and the changing of laws favoring small groups over the majority offer protection and what was lacking in the past: individual empowerment.[14]

Andrew Ash of the Gatestone Institute indicates that

> identity politics, with its emphasis on coercing sympathy and rewarding what often appears a fabricated victimhood, has given way to devaluing, if not ignoring, real victimhood. Identity politics has also possibly caused otherwise sympathetic people to adopt a far more militant position than they otherwise might have taken. . . . One view does not always sit happily alongside another. This is true "diversity," and to the Thought Police, a calamity.[15]

This empowerment has energized certain numeric minorities in America's flipped society to force people to restrict their freedom of speech and that the mere implication of a word can lead to a very public dustup.[16] Others have been shamed in public and on the Internet, while still others are physically attacked. There is a zero-tolerance and a no-compromise attitude that has led some small groups to anger, lawsuits, and personal attacks against those unwilling or unable to concede their own personal and contrary beliefs.

Doxing online postings, which are then shared publicly to spread hurtful secrets or lies in order to compromise one's reputation, is increasing. Spreading of information to embarrass and expose private matters to public eyes is a gang tactic meant to shame and has become a pastime for trolls and people seeking to cause irreparable harm to others.

Schools are soft targets for cliques and bullies seeking to take down those with opposing views. Both teachers and students are targets of doxing. There is a certain militancy on the parts of some small groups at school that take bullying to new levels by ways of smartphones and other devices that appear to shield identities.

A recent summary of National Crime Victimization Statistics revealed that students are cyberbullying at rates higher than in the recent past. The summary revealed that "20 percent of the surveyed students ages 12–18 reported being bullied during the 2016–2017 school year"[17] and that most of this bullying occurred "online or through text messages."[18]

Technology Toxicity

The increase in online and smartphone bullying is reflected in about a 5 percent increase in overall bullying, and the percentage continues to increase. Schools and parents are reluctant to reverse the policies that now enable classrooms to be less literate by smartphone access. This is particularly true in middle and high schools.

Students now only read characters, but prefer photos, videos, and emoticons for communication.[19] In fact, smartphones in the classroom are more likely to be centers of distraction and imminent conduits leading to emotional outbursts. Along with other factors, smart technology has helped our schools dumb down students, on the one hand, yet increase social awareness and activism on the other.[20] In general terms, America is losing its academic prowess in favor of making disciples for social causes.

Smartphones now overwhelm many public schools, with some being used as learning devices by a few savvy teachers. However, the reality is that far too many students resort to what is coined *technology toxicity*. Technology toxicity is the use of technology to capture and distribute words, videos, graphics, pictures, emoticons, and websites that are meant to bully and control others for the purpose of negative or incendiary results. For example, some teachers are secretly recorded in classrooms. Students record other students in compromising situations. Technology has become toxic because it has become weaponized by those with nefarious deeds in mind.[21]

Selective Toxicity
Schools are now places where certain words are off-limits, only for some. In schools, where there is supposed to be an acceptance of differences, some differences are unacceptable, if not outright cultural heresy. Agreement with teachers' neo-toxic views ranks students as tolerant, accepting, and lovingly progressive. Disagreement with teachers' views brings negative labels.

An illustration of *selective toxicity* is demonstrated in the recent actions of the editors of a student newspaper at Palo Alto High School, in Palo Alto, California. As a tradition, the high school newspaper celebrated its college-bound graduating seniors with a list of their names and a map showing their names along with the colleges they would be attending for the following year.[22]

The newspaper editors refused to uphold the tradition stating "though it's intended purpose was to celebrate the post-graduation plans of every senior, the reality is the map contributes to the toxic, comparison-driven culture at Paly."[23] In addition, the editors claimed their community "fosters a college-centric mindset which erodes one's sense of value and can lead students with less traditional plans feeling judged, embarrassed or underrepresented.... this worldview sets the bar for achievement extremely high and punishes anyone who falls short."[24]

In the pursuit to avoid the possibility of offense toward one group, the editors of the school newspaper broke tradition and decided to selectively punish those whose futures included celebrating college admission. The long-standing tradition was deemed toxic by the editors. However, the actions taken by the editors were toxic.

Declaring something toxic that focuses on academics and then replacing it with something negating this focus is an example of the social agency that all too often is applied in schools today. People are no longer allowed to have the opportunity to feel good about themselves if it makes others feel bad in the process.

Religious Toxicity
The practice of one's faith is largely unacceptable in classrooms, unless its practice is tied to a more progressive and tolerant religious faction. In progressivism, there is an active intolerance of timeless truths, for truth does not change as culture changes. As a result, progressives find it difficult to abide by status quo and truth claims from previous generations.

Teachers who hold to either Orthodox Judaism or Evangelical Christianity are assumed to have beliefs in conflict with modern culture and are told to leave their beliefs at the classroom door. However, there are open arms for other religions.

Two decades after the terrorist attack on September 11, 2001, there has been a softening of Muslim acrimony toward those living in America. Although there remains a level of toxicity toward Muslims,[25] in general, public schools are working hard for Muslim inclusiveness in America. Americans are largely tolerant and generous. The more familiar Americans are with Muslims and Islam, the more accepting they may become.[26] The more there is any association of Muslims with terrorism, the greater the marginalization across the wider swath of American culture.

Religious clothing is allowed to be worn in schools, at least for some. Head coverings are worn for religious expression but baseball caps are not. In a secular society, students wonder why certain expressions of allegiance must be tempered while others are not. Schools are not mosques or churches, yet religious attire is allowed. However, if schools are viewed as places of secular religious institutions, then culturally secular and worshipful attire should be acceptable. By favoring one group over another, schools show favoritism, and a toxic environment is established. Selective toxicity frustrates students because it is exclusive.

Another example is found in the allowance of Eastern meditation, which is meant as a method to calm students. In fact, Yoga, which is not just meant for exercise, is encouraged as a way to bring students under control. Students wishing to recite prayers aloud or gathering in the corner for prayer may somehow be in violation, but Yoga and meditational breathing that is expected on behalf of the whole class is not. *This is another example of selective toxicity.*

An Eastern religious practice that is allowed in class, or even led by a teacher—but prayer and reading one's scriptures are not allowed—is again selective and toxic. Therefore, a teacher leading a meditation as part of social-emotional learning may well be violating other students' rights.

Teachers must remember that schools' missions are to educate the whole child. However, given today's educational and cultural climates, this had better take into consideration the ways of Judaism and Christianity, if they take into consideration any religious practice at all.

As culture becomes more antagonistic toward Christianity and Judaism, these two faith traditions are becoming more toxic and persecuted by antagonists. Ironically, as empathy toward Islam grows in American culture, the majority of progressives overlook its historic teachings and cultural practices concerning marriage, treatment of women, and executions of the LGBTQ+ faction.

Schools should not be about selecting favorites. By virtue of such actions, they exclude others, which leads to toxic environments. Schools must focus on academics and the virtues of developing very good readers, excellent mathematicians, and outstanding thinkers. These transcend religious disagreements.

Political Toxicity
Politics have become so polarized and vengeful that anger levels always seem at fever pitch. The mere mention of a political figure is enough to raise the temperature in a room full of students whose views usually reflect those of their parents. Consider that hatred and violence have increased because of the wearing of red hats with slogans.[27] Some have called the *Make American Great Again* hats akin to new white hoods of racists.[28]

That language is itself toxic, but not everyone agrees with political pundits and advocacy journalists about this.[29] However, to those offended by the MAGA hats or Trump's rhetoric, for them each represents something more toxic in their minds.[30] Racist, or not. Either way, politics in the twenty-first century is highly toxic.

An example of hardline side taking was epitomized at a 2019 political rally, where President Trump announced his bid for a second term. Supporters in the audience held up signs, which eventually caused CNN to pack up their cameras and leave. The phrase "CNN Sucks" was one of the evening's showings of the toxic expressions that persist across the political landscape in America.

President Trump has succeeded in cultivating toxicity and marginalizing the media, particularly by his use of the term *fake news*. Teachers in schools all over America are now having to spend time teaching what is and what is not propaganda, fake, or biased reporting.

Each election cycle seems to bring out new levels of extremism, in both rhetoric and actions. The hatred or violence that results is not merely isolated to one political party or one demographic.[31]

When the vitriol of the general public and voting electorate finds its way into the classrooms of America's schools with similar intensity, it is time to step back to reflect on what has been created. Students have been attacked in class by fellow students and teachers and verbally assaulted by both[32] because of opposite political philosophies and the cultivation of toxic environments.[33] Politics has always been controversial, but twenty-first-century disagreements have given way to politics of personal and group destruction.[34]

Marriage and Family as Toxic
People are in serious disagreement over gender issues and changes in marriage definitions. These disagreements have done little to unite the nation. They cause serious effects upon schools and students. Teachers and families are caught between shifts in the cultural foundations of the nation and their school districts advancing positions contrary to personal views. Even though the pressure is on teachers not only to accept new definitions of marriage but to teach them as equals,[35] the federal government has provided guidance for teachers who are asked their opinions by students on issues such as same-sex marriage, abortion, divorce, and other issues.[36]

Teachers can be dismissed from their classroom employment if they do not comply with state curriculum and policy mandates.[37] When teachers feel they are pressured to promote any cultural change, often without the parents' permission, they feel caught in a very disturbing toxic environment. Some teachers are not vocal about their disagreement because of a stigma that comes with disagreeing on certain issues. Rather than deal with such a toxic environment, some teachers just move on to other schools or leave the classrooms altogether.[38]

Classrooms in some locales have become mission fields to counter what teachers perceive as toxic teachings. But the reality is these teachings can come either by the progressives or the traditionalists. By doing so, these actions are labeled offensive and produce a toxicity of their own.

The neo-toxic reality that results from forced cultural changes is "refusing to hear anything that might offend one is not a choice, but a right. Why argue with creatures who have an opposing view when you can simply shut them down?"[39] This is where a marginalized nation demonstrates tyranny.

Gender and Identity Toxicity

A growing number of teachers and college professors are no longer referring to mothers and fathers, men and women, or even boys or girls. In more progressive regions of the nation, educators have adopted new ways to identify people. In some school districts, teachers who refuse to refer to a name chosen by a student—usually one that does not appear on the student rolls or district registration—can be disciplined or even fired, depending on the school district and the extent of progressive local body politic and newer state laws associated with gender identity. For example, "a former central Indiana teacher . . . lost his job after citing religious reasons for disagreeing with a policy compelling teachers to call transgender students by their preferred names rather than birth names"[40] and had to sue his former school district for infringing on his First Amendment religious rights.[41]

One of the reasons that gender and sexuality are so toxic in today's schools is because far too many experts without science credentials are drawing conclusions based on their assumptions and then expecting others to fall in line. Non-experts and supporters of gender and sexual expressions base their conclusions on feelings and social interactions, rather than biology and science.

Children are not mature enough to make life-altering identity proclamations. This is a biological fact. Likewise, parents are unwilling to allow certain progressive ideologies to step into their family networks and declare them unfit parents for shaping the gender of their children. Pop experts have garnered the attention of the media. Along with working with LGBTQ+ lobbies, the small percentage of those claiming a new but toxic truth about gender are content to call the shots for over fifty million students and their families.

Masculinity and Femininity as Toxic

Every so often, a mass shooting devastates a community, and emotions cry out to do something about guns. In the aftermath of such shootings, "some of the more perverse ideas about gender"[42] rise to the surface in society. Colleen Clemens, associate professor of non-Western literatures and director of Women's and Gender Studies at Kutztown University in Pennsylvania writes,

> Seeking an explanation for the mass shootings that happen at a rate of almost one per day in the United States, we have to get away from the idea that "men are just naturally violent." Instead, we need to recognize statements like this as manifestations of "toxic masculinity," and we need to push back against these ideas and the ideology behind them.[43]

Masculinity is under fire today and has been made into its own toxic category. There are various definitions of what toxic masculinity looks like when expressed in daily life. Just as with white privilege and racism, the accusation is that masculinity is so toxic below the surface that it is just part of average boys and men. The idea behind this latent toxicity is stated as "Toxic masculinity [is] the idea that there is only one way to 'be a man'—strong, tough, unfeeling, and aggressive."[44]

In order to disrupt gender norms in the classroom, Clemens suggests people "need to stop telling the boys and the men in our lives to 'man up' when they dare to show emotions or pain. We need to encourage them to drop the 'tough guise' and let them grow up with space for tenderness."[45]

In terms of public schools, Clemens advocates for the creation of "space for boys to know that there is more than one path to becoming a man, and that those paths do not have to lead to violence. We need to teach them that boys are not destined for aggression. To do so, we will need to stay vigilant and persistent in our conversations about gender."[46]

There are some concerns with sweeping opinions like those held by Clemens. Such opinions have no room for opposing viewpoints. Such opinions also steer clear of the ethnic and racial cultures that comprise American society, of which men are clearly a part. For example, is it possible that any notion of toxic masculinity is a problem to some authors because of European roots? What about Middle Eastern masculinity or Asian masculinity? Are these not also toxic?

Progressive American scholars conveniently leave out non-Caucasian demographics in addressing toxicity and place the blame on descendants of White, Eurocentric forebears. One has to question whether toxic femininity is soon to be bound to the same fundamental assumptions. See chapter 5 for an extensive discussion on toxic masculinity.

Traditional American Roles as Toxic
Sometimes, what is labeled as toxic masculinity is actually a social adjustment or, more colloquially, as *stepping up to the plate*. Men and women through the ages have defended their families by any and all means necessary. Today, masculinity is responsible for fathers defending their children against having their reputations ruined online. Furthermore, throughout history, masculinity has also been responsible for hunters killing animals for food and going to war against other nations as well as being an important part of the gifted athlete's competitive pouncing on opponents' weaknesses.

In a culture that ranges from survival to ultra-competitive, schools and businesses have experienced masculinity to their advantage. Our nation has arrived at lowering men into a place that is defined mostly by women and elevating women by the same. There is a reason for this. The moment men begin to define masculinity or femininity, they earn the toxic label of *misogynists*.[47]

Fortunately, not everyone views the current trend of labeling young men the same way.[48] There are different voices, even among some in Hollywood. Actress Meryl Streep writes: "We hurt our boys by calling something toxic masculinity.... Women can be pretty ... toxic people. We have our good angles and we have our bad ones. I think the labels are less helpful than what we are trying to get to, which is communication, direct, between human beings. We're all on the boat together. We've got to make it work."[49]

The theories of toxic masculinity are not "only relegated to women's studies classes and online harassment. The specific kind of toxicity Streep is talking about involves a kind of hyper-gendered behavior. It's not saying outright that men are evil or inherently violent. The danger today involves people misinterpreting the term and assuming that it covers things such as violence and misogyny."[50]

What is often missing from critiques such as Streep's is that, in a nation of polarized opposites politically, both sides practice similar tactics. When Streep was named as a winner of the Cecil B. DeMille Award at the 74th Golden Globes, she encouraged an escalation of toxicity by pleading with the media in attendance. "As she accepted her prize, the star urged members of the media to hold Trump accountable for his words and actions. And she slammed him for his behavior on the campaign trail, specifically toward journalists."[51]

Streep went on the offensive to criticize the president while she did so from a type of powerful platform. Hers was another form of a bully pulpit, all on national television. Toxic is as toxic does. Streep is accurate when she concludes disrespect invites disrespect and words of violence invite violence. Again, both political extremes see this toxicity play out across the nation. As always, children are paying attention.

Doyin Richards inscribes three ways to combat toxic masculinity and shares the rationale and priority for doing so. "Breaking down these assumptions about how boys especially should act—often referred to as 'toxic masculinity'—should be a priority for every parent.... there are three main ideas needed to dismantle this dynamic."[52]

Richards's advises diffusion and rejection of any notion that there are such things as boy things and girl things. "As long as they aren't hurting anyone in the process, there's nothing inherently wrong with children embracing their authentic selves.... If a boy wants to wear a tutu, let him. If a girl wants to roll around in the mud with a football, let her." This marginalizes parents as bad parents for not conforming to a self-avowed feminist's understanding of masculinity.[53] According to Richards, "Sometimes we have to risk offending people to make the world a better place."[54] However, this does not cut both ways.

States as Toxic

Recently, the state of New Jersey instructed schools to use the "preferred pronouns and names of trans-identified students and provide for them access to bathrooms, locker rooms and showers that match their gender identity."[55] As a counterargument, a belief considered toxic to those of the LGBTQ+ community, is best summed up by Ken Ham, founder of *Answers in Genesis*. Ham states that "to teach true equality and inclusion would require teaching that all humans are made in God's image . . . all are sinners, all can receive the true gift of salvation, and all need to judge their behavior/worldview against the absolute standard—God's Holy Word."[56]

Several states are pressing forward with what some parental groups claim is indoctrination and usurpation of parental instruction of their children.[57] Bills are being passed that advocate for LGBTQ+-inclusive curricula for students at every level. Supporters of this movement say that "such lessons expose students to a more inclusive and accurate account of history and promotes acceptance and diversity,"[58] bringing into alignment classroom materials "with the states core curriculum standards by ensuring that students receive diverse instruction in history and the social sciences."[59]

Common Core State Standards continue to remain toxic in the minds of the general public.[60] Judith Butler, professor at the University of California, Berkeley, writes that

> the idea . . . "male" and "female" are merely social constructs . . . "because gender is not a fact, the various acts of gender create the idea of gender, and without those acts, there would be no gender at all."
>
> Butler is a professor of comparative literature, not a neuroscientist or psychologist, but her ideas about gender have become widely accepted worldwide in the nearly 30 years since the publication of her book, *Gender Trouble*.[61]

Cordella Fine, "professor of historical and philosophical studies at the University of Melbourne, published a book titled *Testosterone Rex: Unmaking the Myths of Our Gendered Minds*. Following Butler, Fine asserted that any claims that women and men differ significantly in brain or behavior are simply myths perpetuated by the heteronormative patriarchy."[62]

Both Butler's and Fine's books have been given majestic critical acclaim, despite being published as nonscientists. The current sociological and psychological pressure in American culture to compromise biology and science is immense.[63] One thing is clear. The trend away from anything that smacks of traditional understanding of gender and sex seems insurmountable.

The fact is that anyone claiming scientific knowledge that counters the trend of all things LGBTQ+, as well as the social construct theory, is not given a fair hearing.[64] The only outcome in dealing with disagreements over sex and gender is a complete shutdown of dissent. Both extremes are quite intolerant of the other side's positions.[65]

The worldview promulgated by Butler, Fine, and their followers now constrains what some scientists are allowed to say in public. This punitive action is not just found in the United States. For example,

> a professor of neurophysiology at Lund University in Sweden recently told undergraduates that categories of male and female are, to some degree, biological realities rather than social constructs and that some differences in behavior between women and men might, therefore, have a biological basis. He was promptly denounced by students who claimed his remarks were "anti-feminist."[66]

The fact that science has spoken a different version of the facts is unacceptable and toxic to progressives because such views do not square with other claims on gender and sexuality. Whatever happened to reasoned debate? One version of science is dismissed out of hand because of claims that studies are affected by the social constructs. One scientist labeled as toxic is Leonard Sax, a physician and researcher.

Sax, who has debated disciples of Butler and Fine over the issues of gender construct versus scientific fact, encourages more debate. He posits the following:

> So let's study humans before *birth*. In recent years, there have been fascinating studies in which neuroscientists have studied the brains of babies in their mothers' wombs. One remarkable study was a collaboration among scientists at Yale, Johns Hopkins, and the National Institute of Mental Health, alongside neuroscientists from Germany, the UK, Croatia, and Portugal—more than 20 researchers in all. These investigators looked at how individual genes are transcribed in the human brain from the prenatal period through infancy, childhood, adolescence, and throughout adulthood. They found that the biggest female/male difference in gene transcription in the human brain, for many genes, is in the prenatal period. The transcription of the IGF2 gene, a gene known to be involved in cognition: male/female differences in transcription for IGF2 are huge in the prenatal period, and nonexistent among adults. . . . If the Butler/Fine theory was correct—if gendered differences in brain and behavior are primarily a social construct, and not hardwired—then we ought

to see zero differences between the female brain and the male brain in the prenatal period, but large differences between adults, who after all have had the misfortune of living all their lives in a heteronormative patriarchy. But the reality is just the opposite: Female/male differences are generally largest in the prenatal period, and those differences diminish with age, often dwindling to zero among adults.[67]

Sax goes on to say:

> Now we have another, even more striking study of the human brain prior to birth. In this study, American researchers managed to do MRI scans of pregnant mothers in the second and third trimesters, with sufficient resolution to image the brains of the babies inside the uterus. They found dramatic differences between female and male fetuses. For example, female fetuses demonstrated significant changes in connectivity between subcortical and cortical structures in the brain, as a function of gestational age. This pattern "was almost completely non-existent in male fetuses." They note that others have found, for example, that female infants have significantly greater brain volume in the prefrontal cortex compared with males. They conclude that "It seems likely that these volumetric differences [found after birth] are mirrored by [the] differences observed in the present study." . . . Remember, these are fetuses in utero! In other brain areas, the differences were not so striking. A reasonable next question might be: Why do these brain areas, and not others, show such dramatic female/male differences? A reasonable question would be: Why haven't the mainstream media in the United States covered this new research?[68]

There is a toxic environment, and it is maintained as such by the LGBTQ+ lobbies. Some science is kept at arm's length, while other studies are accepted as fact. The implications for teachers on brain differences and gender are enormous. Not only do teachers battle with what to do with their own personal views, but they have to decide whether they will teach what is contrary to all they have ever known about themselves.

Generally, teachers have a basic common sense and practical knowledge regarding true differences in boys and girls. Their learning styles, energy levels, and the ways they view the world are quite evident—long before any social constructs are foisted upon each of them.

No one knows all the facts on any topic, especially with unique beings such as humans. But should everyone not be free to be heard on a topic?

Free Speech as Toxic

Allan M. Josephson, former chief of the Division of Child and Adolescent Psychiatry at the University of Louisville, "participated on a youth gender dysphoria panel in 2017, at the Heritage Foundation. He was released from his position at the university, due to his positions on gender dysphoria. Josephson contended that 'it's impossible to speak about gender identity without thinking of the parent-child relationship.'"[69] He went on to say that "children do not know a whole lot yet at the age of seven to nine," and suggested that it is too young for them to pick a gender identity. "We are going to let them at the age of eight or nine decide that they're no longer a male or female? . . . Unbelievable."[70]

The punishment for speaking out in disagreement in challenging anything LGBTQ+ can have devastating effects on a person's career.

> After the Heritage panel was posted online, UL's LGBT Center, "sounded the alarm," and officials there "were troubled at the views Dr. Josephson expressed." . . . The division chief was then met with swift backlash for what he had said on the panel, and a few of his colleagues demanded that the university discipline him. . . . UL then demoted Josephson to a junior faculty position after the incident . . . and the university decided not to renew his contract.[71]

This shows the stranglehold that just a few people have over the messaging to which all of academe must submit or face consequences. This is the toxic environment in which academe finds itself across many disciplines. Free speech in society is all but dead. Free speech is intolerable when it communicates ideas contrary to the LGBTQ+ status quo. The only times speech is considered free is when the speech toes the line of the progressive social agenda. In addition to the toxicity around gender and sex, the issue of race is equally as toxic today. All of these toxins are affecting students in America's public schools.

Systemic Racism as Toxic
H. Richard Milner states

> too many educators today covertly or tacitly believe racism has ended in schools and society. They may inaccurately believe that racism is solely a function of individual acts, and because they do not believe they (as individuals) commit racist acts, they fail to understand that racism exists on the individual, systemic, institutional, and structural levels. . . . So when we think of student mental health in schools, some may not even consider the insidious effects of racism that students of color experience.[72]

Milner adds,

> But race is about far more than skin color. Race is constructed physically, contextually, socially, legally, and historically. And it is inextricably linked

to patterns of prejudice and power structures. . . . I have found in my research that, despite the best intentions, white teachers may develop and enact curriculum and instructional practices that contribute to inequity and harmful racial assumptions.[73]

Drilling down more deeply into issues often brings new light to issues and deeper understanding.

It is possible for people to make comments and hold beliefs that imply something racial, but not racist. However, in so doing, "some students experience what are known as racial micro-aggressions, 'brief and commonplace daily verbal, behavioral, or environmental indignities, whether intentional or unintentional, that communicate hostile, derogatory, or negative racial slights and insults toward people of color.'"[74]

Students may experience racial micro-aggressions inside or outside of school, but either way, the experiences can affect their mental outlook as students. In their research on higher education,

> McGee and Stovall (2015) found that uncomfortable, unwelcoming, stressful, and hostile campus climates can take a toll on students of color and result in health challenges that can ultimately influence their performance in classes. Moreover, these researchers linked racism and discrimination to anxiety, stress, depression, thoughts of suicide, and physical ailments like hair loss, diabetes, and heart disease.[75]

There is now a model of acceptability to accuse people of racism, even as no one is able to read the motivations of minds and hearts. How long will it be before a balding or depressed person sues because his or her maladies are supposedly linked to having to listen to perceived racial rhetoric?

Universities are teaching that there are certain privileges that are part of a systemic racist culture in America and that this racist ideology exists in the majority of people and institutions in America. Again, as with the issues of gender and sex, there is no arguing or disagreement tolerated by those views. The very nature of the disagreement—even if done with respect and research—is called out with predictable bravura as examples of the privilege and bigotry that people are certain already exist.

The following is an example pieced together from conversations heard on college campuses and in general conversations in public. There is a certain general refrain presented. The dialogue begins with a premise upon which both sides agree and ends with a summary conclusion.

Premise: America is a nation where we have free speech!

Person 1: I do not like what you just said, and you should be ashamed.

Person 2: Are you gaslighting me? (*Gaslighting is manipulating a person by psychological tactics so that he or she questions his or her own views, truth, memories, perceptions, or even sanity.*)

Person 1: No, just using my freedom to tell you how I feel.

Person 2: I take that as a micro-aggression, and you do not have that right.

Person 1: I can say whatever I feel.

Person 2: You only feel that way because of pervasive cultural latent bias and privilege.

Person 1: That's crazy.

Person 2: Only an insensitive person would say that.

Person 1: Whatever happened to free speech?

Person 2: Nothing, but you can't micro-aggress, gaslight, or imply anything that makes anyone feel like they have been offended.

Person 1: Why not? What if what you just said offends me?

Person 2: You can't be offended; you do not have a history of oppression like I do. You are capable of hurting others only because of your privilege.

Person 1: That is just plain stupid.

Person 2: See, there you go again offending me.

Person 1: How, by disagreeing?

Person 2: You are a racist down deep, and you do not even know it.

Conclusion: Free speech belongs to only those who claim they have freedom to say as they please and accuse as they please. Their views must be right because they say so and they are smarter. Calling out "shame," which, if done to those calling it out, would be deemed gaslighting and offensive, is a reverse tactic to limit free speech, not allow it. Toxicity in culture is caused by people, and either we have freedom of speech and tolerate the disagreements, or we do not. Nothing is solved by marginalizing and name-calling.

Diversity Training as Toxic

In the twenty-first century, race remains a central issue for some, even though national polls seem to indicate that Americans have moved on to other pressing issues.[76] Where race remains front and center, school districts either have evidence of it or assume it is an underlying reality. In either case, school districts have taken to doing more in the creation of learning environments for students while spending many hours training teachers in ways to understand and apply their understanding of diversity.

UCLA professor of education, Tyrone Howard, suggests several ways to go about developing better racial climates on school campuses.[77] Howard shares, "five tenets to disrupt racist thinking and practices."[78] These tenets include:

- One-time diversity professional development is not enough.
- Leaders need to lead.
- Bystanders need to speak up.
- Racially diverse staff must be heard.
- Parents and students deserve a say.

In some states, teachers receive training on ways to move forward on race. For example,

> In controversial "implicit bias" training, New York City's public-school educators have been told to focus on black children over white ones—and one Jewish superintendent who described her family's Holocaust tragedies was scolded and humiliated, according to firsthand accounts. A consultant hired by the city Department of Education told administrators at a workshop that "racial equity" means favoring black children regardless of their socio-economic status.[79]

According to Darnisa Amante, a Harvard lecturer and educational consultant hired by the New York City Department of Education (NYC DOE) to conduct a mandatory training:

> If I had a poor white male student and I had a middle-class black boy, I would actually put my equitable strategies and interventions into that middle-class black boy because over the course of his lifetime he will have less access and less opportunities than that poor white boy.... That is what racial equity is.... Through this process of moving towards racial equity, we will have to pull layers back on who we are. You are going to have to talk about your power and your privilege.... You are going to have to acknowledge that you will have to step back. You might fear losing your job. When we get to true racial equity you will have to define new institutional policies. This might feel dangerous because you are going to have to talk about race daily.[80]

NYC DOE spokesman Will Mantell added: "Anti-bias and equity trainings are about creating high expectations and improving outcomes for all of our students."[81] When racial equality means toxic inequality it is probably time to rethink the strategy.

Not all agree that the problems being addressed by the training were done fairly and met the needs of all teachers for all students.

> The DOE's anti-bias training—a $23 million mandatory program for all DOE employees—has irked some administrators, teachers, and parents who contend parts are ugly and divisive. Four white female DOE executives demoted under NYC school chancellor Richard Carranza, "plan to sue the city for racial discrimination, claiming whiteness has become 'toxic.'"[82]

Another example of a toxic environment that can be created by diversity training includes a Manhattan middle-school teacher,

> with her own kids in public schools. She complained that "the DOE training is a 'catalyst for hate and division.' I have colleagues who won't participate during 'Courageous Conversations' (the DOE protocol for implicit-bias workshops) because they do not feel safe." The teacher reiterated that she "cringes at training phrases like 'replacement thinking' and the disdain for 'whiteness.'"[83]

Those who criticized the training were guilty of carrying the same latent racial biases as others across the nation. In fact, "'those who do not see the value in this work are the ones who must look inward harder,' said Shino Tanikawa, a parent in Manhattan's District 2 and member of Mayor de Blasio's School Diversity Advisory Group."[84] Programs meant to focus on one problem that is defined as systemic can often lead to other problems that become as problematic as the original. When this happens the result is a toxic environment.

Under the umbrella of diversity, policies that focus on students of color may become toxic to the very students these policies are meant to assist. For instance, racial profiling has been used to dissuade schools from disciplining students of color for fear that an inordinate number of students would be placed into a pipeline of trouble. Moreover, discipline policies that yielded higher numbers of suspended and expelled students, when compared to Caucasian students, were deemed racist, hence, the birth of programs such as restorative justice circles and in-school suspensions.

The guidance for the current programs in discipline programs originated in the Obama administration. Advocates of social justice view discipline of students of color as moving students "further down school-to-prison pipeline with every school suspension."[85] This led to a middle position of in-school suspensions, and the thinking is that keeping such students in school "may be a key shut-off valve."[86]

Diversity no longer applies to only traditional, basic demographic categories. Those with special needs and anyone who self-identifies with a special need or with a gender difference is now included under any diversity umbrella. For example, along with the rise in autism, emotional disorders, and physical disabilities, there is now a category for those with *Oppositional Defiant Disorder*. Classrooms with students who have ODD make it "incredibly frustrating for teachers, who are often already dealing with a variety of behavioral issues that are usual in kids anyway."[87]

States have added new categories and subcategories to their special education programs, and nearly every student in public education in those states can find a qualifying placement under one heading or another. For example, "the disability categories and enrollment breakdown in California for individuals (newborn through twenty-two years of age) who received special education services in 2018–19"[88] included:

- Autism: 120,095
- Deaf-blindness: 114
- Deafness: 3,233
- Emotional disturbance: 25,233
- Hard of hearing: 10,657
- Intellectual disabilities: 43,770
- Multiple disabilities: 7,308
- Orthopedic impairment: 9,916
- Other health impairment: 104,792
- Specific learning disability: 300,295
- Speech or language impairment: 164,698
- Traumatic brain injury: 1,541
- Visual impairment: 3,405

Within each of these major categories, there are spectra, subcategories, and qualifications that enable eligibility. From ages 3–22, there were just under eight hundred thousand students in California's schools who received special education services within the 2018–2019 school year.[89]

Special Services as Toxic

Over the course of several years, the question of inordinate application of discipline has also been asked about students of color, in terms of their placement into special education classes. The question is two-pronged and has been asked, "Are black and Hispanic students identified for special education too often, or not often enough?"[90]

Already established federal regulations "require districts to guard against greatly over-identifying minority students with disabilities—also known as 'significant disproportionality' in the regulations of the Individuals with Disabilities Education Act (IDEA). Nationally, 14 percent of white students ages 3–21 are in special education; for black students it is 16 percent and for Hispanic students, 13 percent."[91]

Today, there are so many circumstances that children face that fall under one or more categories of special education services. Certainly, there is no mistaking the fact that poverty is a factor correlated with children receiving special education services in public schools.[92] As government includes more designations of special services, the numbers of students who fit these new categories are added, making numbers of special services swell under the heading of special education services.[93]

The University of Kansas, School of Education, put together a timeline of changes and additions to special education services identified by the Individuals with Disabilities Education Act. Beginning with *Brown v. Board of Topeka Kansas* (1954) and continuing through President Johnson's 1965 Elementary and Secondary Education Act (ESEA) and the 2004 Congressional amended Individuals with Disabilities Education Act, called for

> early intervention for students, greater accountability and improved educational outcomes, and raised the standards for instructors who teach special education classes. It also required states to demand that local school districts shift up to 15 percent of their special education funds toward general education if it were determined that a disproportionate number of students from minority groups were placed in special education for reasons other than disability.[94]

Sports as Toxic

Calm and relaxed parents can sometimes become agitated—and even unrecognizable—when incidents involving their children occur at school. Sometimes, agitation turns excessive when it comes to sports-related activities. The fact is that competition sometimes brings out the best and worst of human behaviors, and not just among the on-field competitors.

Americans live at a time when parents are pressing their children to play sports. There is so much pressure placed on children today at younger and younger ages to play sports year-round. The environment to compete and win is taking its toll on athletes. More and more athletes are tearing ligaments in elbows and knees and breaking bones while finding ways to win at all cost. The pressure to compete and win at all cost has created a toxic sports environment for parents, athletes, coaches, and even game officials.

Parents in the stands at games are sometimes unruly, screaming obscenities at referees and umpires. The horrible part is when an already emotional environment turns toxic. Circumstances can turn ugly and physical confrontations can occur. The following is a case in point. At an elementary school in Colorado, some parents did not like the calls of a 13-year-old umpire as he umpired a game for 7-year-olds. As a result, about "15–20 adults got into a violent tussle."[95] Several citations were handed out by police and there were injuries, including one person who "suffered serious bodily injury."[96]

Sports at every level are becoming more and more toxic. The recent scandals revealed the favoritism and buying of children's admission to elite colleges and universities. The nepotism for famous political figures demonstrates another aspect of toxicity on college campuses, as some students complain that some students gain entrance into some of the nation's best institutions of higher education only because of donations, political connections, or certain quid pro quo.[97]

Athletics in America add another level of toxicity to schools, clubs, and colleges, and this toxicity affects all age groups and men's and women's sports. Recently, transgender athletes have competed in sports competitions according to their chosen gender, rather than their birth gender. This upset many parents and competitors, making an already toxic environment even more toxic, in terms of all the competitors, parents, and those athletes left out because of rule changes.[98]

Toxicity is a very real problem in America, and it affects everyone at some point. Whether in schools, in the workplace, on the athletic field, or just out and about, wherever humans gather, toxicity also exists. However, in this twenty-first-century neo-toxic era, people are being informed that (1) as people, they are toxic and do not even know it, or (2) they know it and refuse to deal with it. The implications for teachers is that to focus on academics over social-emotional learning is racist. When teachers are told they treat their students in different ways and are not aware of this, the guilt of implicit bias is placed heavily upon them and often interferes with their ability to relax and do their jobs. Teachers may be racists unknowingly.

Also in this neo-toxic era, government officials would like to exercise more control and force public educators and parents to knuckle under and abide by constraints placed on them—especially those who may dissent. What government officials do not realize, or maybe do not care about, is the fact that their laws and policies have created a large portion of the neo-toxic environment and, by the illogical misapplication of true toxicity, have created sub-neo-toxic categories, into which most Americans are placed.

The only exceptions that exist in American culture and fall outside of the toxic label are self-exceptions. The crafters of the neo-toxic categories and the eventual punishments for dissent are exempt from judgment. The bottom line is that, by politically motivated efforts, those in the neo-toxic power structure, by their efforts to void toxicity, have established for most Americans the very thing they had endeavored to remove.

Notes

1. Andrew Ash. "The unsafe space of the first day of school." *Gatestone Institute*. August 26, 2019. Retrieved from https://www.gatestoneinstitute.org/14561/unsafe-spaces.

2. Brittney Beck. "We must nurture youth activism in Kern." *The Bakersfield Californian*. September 24, 2019. Retrieved from https://www.bakersfield.com/opinion/community-voices-we-must-nurture-youth-activism-in-kern/article_e9b53224-de36-11e9-9e80-a729715eaeb0.html.

3. Megan Zahneis. "White-supremacist propaganda on campuses rose 77% last year." *The Chronicle of Higher Education*. June 28, 2018. Retrieved from https://www.chronicle.com/article/White-Supremacist-Propaganda/243786. Cf. Jonathan M. Metzl. *Dying of whiteness: How the politics of racial resentment is killing America's heartland*. 2019. New York: Basic Books.

4. Bianca Padro Ocasio. "Police group director: Obama caused a 'war on cops.'" *Politico*. July 8, 2016. Retrieved from https://www.politico.com/story/2016/07/obama-war-on-cops-police-advocacy-group-225291.

5. William Cummings. "Conservatives fire back at Obama, say he sowed the division that led to Trump." *USA Today*. September 10, 2018. Retrieved from https://www.usatoday.com/story/news/politics/onpolitics/2018/09/10/conservatives-attack-obama-speech/1254935002/.

6. Juliet Eilperin and Darla Cameron. "How Trump is rolling back Obama's legacy." *Washington Post*. March 24, 2017. Retrieved from https://www.washingtonpost.com/graphics/politics/trump-rolling-back-obama-rules/?noredirect=on&utm_term=.43d745fa5626.

7. Megan Zahneis. "White-supremacist propaganda on campuses rose 77% last year."

8. Ibid.

9. Mahita Gajanan. "Texas district moves to fire teacher who tried to report undocumented students to Trump on Twitter." *Time*. June 5, 2019. Retrieved from https://time.com/5601176/fort-worth-teacher-fired-trump-tweets-immigrants/.

10. Aaron Colen. "Texas teacher suspended for reporting illegal immigrant students to Pres. Trump on Twitter." *The Blaze*. May 31, 2019. Retrieved from https://

www.theblaze.com/news/texas-teacher-suspended-for-reporting-illegal-immigrant-students-to-pres-trump-on-twitter. Cf. Mahita Gajanan. "Texas district moves to fire teacher who tried to report undocumented students to Trump on Twitter." *Time.* June 5, 2019. Retrieved from https://time.com/5601176/fort-worth-teacher-fired-trump-tweets-immigrants/.

11. Staff. "White privilege as an influencer." *The Good Men Project.* July 1, 2018. Retrieved from https://goodmenproject.com/featured-content/white-privilege-influencer-lbkr/.

12. Roberta Katz. "How Gen Z is different, according to social scientists (and young people themselves)." *Pacific Standard.* April 2, 2019. Retrieved from https://psmag.com/ideas/how-gen-z-is-different-according-to-social-scientists. Cf. Staff. "Getting Gen Z primed to save the world." *Atlantic.* 2019. Retrieved from https://www.theatlantic.com/sponsored/allstate/getting-gen-z-primed-to-save-the-world/747/.

13. Pritha Paul. "11-year-old allegedly shamed for picking Trump as 'hero' for school project." *International Business Times.* April 4, 2019. Retrieved from https://www.ibtimes.com/11-year-old-allegedly-shamed-picking-trump-hero-school-project-2784578. Cf. Jonathan Zimmerman. "Democracy depends on kids not imitating Donald Trump's racist tweets and attacks." *USA Today.* July 19, 2019. Retrieved from https://www.usatoday.com/story/opinion/2019/07/19/condemn-trump-racism-but-not-students-who-support-him-column/1745220001/.

14. James Kirchick. "The struggle for gay rights is over." *Atlantic.* June 28, 2019. Retrieved from https://www.theatlantic.com/ideas/archive/2019/06/battle-gay-rights-over/592645/.

15. Andrew Ash. "The unsafe space of the first day of school."

16. Abby Koenig. "Is the word faggot still offensive?" *Houston Press.* June 18, 2014. Retrieved from https://www.houstonpress.com/arts/is-the-word-faggot-still-offensive-6394629.

17. Hector Alejandro Arzate. "Cyberbullying is on the rise among teenagers, national survey finds." *Education Week.* July 15, 2019. Retrieved from https://blogs.edweek.org/edweek/District_Dossier/2019/07/cyberbullying_is_on_the_rise_a.html.

18. Ibid.

19. Jeremy Adams. "My high school students don't read anymore. I think I know why." *Los Angeles Times.* August 23, 2019. Retrieved from https://www.latimes.com/opinion/story/2019-08-22/death-of-reading-high-school-cellphone.

20. Ernest J. Zarra III. "Eventually we're going to leave a dumbed-down generation behind." *The Bakersfield Californian.* February 3, 2015. Retrieved from https://www.bakersfield.com/opinion/ernie-zarra-eventually-we-re-going-to-leave-a-dumbed/article_a93412a6-c762-5e4b-95ce-e5fa11ace395.html.

21. Ernest J. Zarra III. *The entitled generation: Helping teachers teach and reach the minds and hearts of Generation Z.* 2017. Lanham, Maryland: Rowman & Littlefield Publishers.

22. John Hasson. "Calif. high school paper slams 'competitive, goal-oriented' mindsets of grads." *Campus Reform.* June 17, 2019. Retrieved from https://www.campusreform.org/?ID=13339.

23. Ibid.

24. Ibid.

25. David Masci. "Many Americans see religious discrimination in U.S.—especially against Muslims." Pew Research Center. May 17, 2019. Retrieved from https://www.pewresearch.org/fact-tank/2019/05/17/many-americans-see-religious-discrimination-in-u-s-especially-against-muslims/.

26. Scott Gardner and Jonathan Evans. "In western Europe, familiarity with Muslims is linked to positive views of Muslims and Islam." Pew Research Center. July 24, 2018. Retrieved from https://www.pewresearch.org/fact-tank/2018/07/24/in-western-europe-familiarity-with-muslims-is-linked-to-positive-views-of-muslims-and-islam/.

27. Deroy Murdock. "The war on red caps roars on." *National Review*. March 20, 2019. Retrieved from https://www.nationalreview.com/2019/03/violence-against-trump-supporters-make-america-great-again-hats/.

28. Isaac Bailey. "Why Trump's MAGA hats have become a potent symbol of racism." CNN. March 12, 2019. Retrieved from https://www.cnn.com/2019/01/21/opinions/maga-hat-has-become-a-potent-racist-symbol-bailey/index.html.

29. Meredith Dost, Ryan D. Enos, and Jennifer L. Hochschild. "Is President Trump's rhetoric racist? It depends on whom you ask." *Washington Post*. August 12, 2019. Retrieved from https://www.washingtonpost.com/politics/2019/08/12/is-president-trumps-rhetoric-racist-it-depends-whom-you-ask/.

30. Matt Ford. "Donald Trump's guide to racism." *The New Republic*. August 13, 2019. Retrieved from https://newrepublic.com/article/154743/donald-trumps-guide-racism.

31. Erik Pedersen. "CNN bails on Donald Trump re-election ray after crowd chants 'CNN Sucks.'" *Yahoo News*. June 18, 2019. Retrieved from https://www.yahoo.com/entertainment/cnn-bails-donald-trump-election-013339914.html.

32. Madison Dibble. "Teacher forces entire class to relocate to get away from a**hole student wearing a MAGA hat." *Independent Journal Review*. November 28, 2018. Retrieved from https://ijr.com/teacher-maga-hat/.

33. Ernest J. Zarra III. *Assaulted: Violence in schools and what needs to be done.* 2018. Lanham, Maryland: Rowman & Littlefield Publishers. Cf. Benjamin Fearnow. "Video shows teacher wrapping Trump 2020 'MAGA' flag around student's head, school investigating." *Newsweek*. March 5, 2019. Retrieved from https://www.newsweek.com/trump-flag-student-maga-neck-york-high-school-teacher-viral-video-1352465.

34. Bruce Drake and Jocelyn Kiley. "Americans say the nation's political debate has grown more toxic and 'heated' rhetoric could lead to violence." Pew Research Center. July 18, 2019. Retrieved from https://www.pewresearch.org/fact-tank/2019/07/18/americans-say-the-nations-political-debate-has-grown-more-toxic-and-heated-rhetoric-could-lead-to-violence/.

35. Doug DuBrin. "Constitutional amendments and same-sex marriage—Lesson plan." *PBS Newshour*. 2019. Retrieved from https://www.pbs.org/newshour/extra/lessons-plans/constitutional-amendments-and-gay-marriage/.

36. Staff. "Good news for teachers: Guidance amended to protect Christian speech on marriage." *Christian Concern*. May 10, 2019. Retrieved from https://www.christianconcern.com/our-issues/education/good-news-for-teachers-guidance-amended-to-protect-christian-speech-on-marriage.

37. Rebecca Klein. "Guide shows teachers how to talk with kids about gay marriage." *Huffington Post*. June 6, 2015. Retrieved from https://www.huffpost.com/entry/gay-marriage-teachers-guide_n_7690244.

38. Ernest J. Zarra III. *The age of teacher shortages: From social agency to academic urgency*. 2019. Lanham, Maryland: Rowman & Littlefield Publishers.

39. Andrew Ash. "The unsafe space of the first day of school." *Gatestone Institute*. August 26, 2019. Retrieved from https://www.gatestoneinstitute.org/14561/unsafe-spaces.

40. Staff. "Ex-teacher sues over ousting over transgender student names." *U.S. News and World Report*. June 22, 2018. Retrieved from https://www.usnews.com/news/best-states/indiana/articles/2019-06-22/ex-teacher-sues-over-ousting-over-transgender-student-names.

41. Staff. "Ex-teacher sues over ousting over transgender student names." *U.S. News and World Report*. June 22, 2018. Retrieved from https://www.usnews.com/news/best-states/indiana/articles/2019-06-22/ex-teacher-sues-over-ousting-over-transgender-student-names.

42. Colleen Clemens. "Toxic masculinity is bad for everyone: Why teachers must disrupt gender norms every day." *Teaching Tolerance*. January 4, 2018. Retrieved from https://www.tolerance.org/magazine/toxic-masculinity-is-bad-for-everyone-why-teachers-must-disrupt-gender-norms-every-day.

43. Ibid.

44. Ibid.

45. Ibid.

46. Ibid.

47. Carrie N. Baker. "The female face of men's misogyny." *Ms*. September 25, 2018. Retrieved from https://msmagazine.com/2018/09/25/female-face-mens-misogyny/. Cf. Nina Renata Aron. "What does misogyny look like?" *New York Times*. March 8, 2019. Retrieved from https://www.nytimes.com/2019/03/08/style/misogyny-women-history-photographs.html.

48. David J. Ley. "Feminists think sexist men are sexier than 'woke' men." *Psychology Today*. December 12, 2018. Retrieved from https://www.psychologytoday.com/us/blog/women-who-stray/201812/feminists-think-sexist-men-are-sexier-woke-men.

49. Christopher Luu. "Meryl Streep doesn't agree with the term 'toxic masculinity.'" *Instyle*. May 30, 2019. Retrieved from https://www.instyle.com/news/meryl-streep-toxic-masculinity.

50. Ibid.

51. Jennifer Earl. "Meryl Streep's politically charged comments, from the Golden Globes to a Colbert-hosted fundraiser." *Fox News*. December 3, 2018. Retrieved

from https://www.foxnews.com/entertainment/meryl-streeps-politically-charged-comments-from-golden-globes-to-colbert-fundraiser.

52. Doyin Richards. "How every parent can help get rid of toxic masculinity." *Mashable*. March 16, 2019. Retrieved from https://mashable.com/article/parents-kids-toxic-masculinity/.

53. Ibid.

54. Ibid.

55. Samuel Smith. "NJ law forcing schools to teach LGBT history is about indoctrinating students, critics say." *Christian Post*. February 12, 2019. Retrieved from https://www.christianpost.com/news/nj-law-forcing-schools-to-teach-lgbt-history-is-about-indoctrinating-students-critics-say.html.

56. Ibid.

57. Ibid.

58. Ibid.

59. Ibid.

60. Ernest J. Zarra III. *The wrong direction for today's schools: The impact of Common Core on American education*. 2015. Lanham, Maryland: Rowman & Littlefield Publishers.

61. Leonard Sax. "A new study blows up old ideas about girls and boys." *Psychology Today*. March 27, 2019. Retrieved from https://www.psychologytoday.com/us/blog/sax-sex/201903/new-study-blows-old-ideas-about-girls-and-boys. Cf. Dino Franco Felluga. *Critical Theory: The Key Concepts*. 2015. New York: Routledge.

62. Ibid.

63. Debra W. Soh. "Science shows sex is binary, not a spectrum." *Real Clear Politics*. October 31, 2018. Retrieved from https://www.realclearpolitics.com/articles/2018/10/31/science_shows_sex_is_binary_not_a_spectrum_138506.html.

64. Caleb Parke. "College student kicked out of class for telling professor there are only two genders." *Fox News*. March 12, 2018. Retrieved from https://www.foxnews.com/us/college-student-kicked-out-of-class-for-telling-professor-there-are-only-two-genders.

65. Wanda Skowronska. "Psychologists who dissent from the reigning gender ideology." *Crisis Magazine*. June 20, 2018. Retrieved from https://www.crisismagazine.com/2018/psychologists-dissent-reigning-gender-ideology.

66. Leonard Sax. "A new study blows up old ideas about girls and boys."

67. Ibid.

68. Ibid.

69. Adam Sabes. "Prof ousted after sharing views on youth gender dysphoria sues." *Campus Reform*. April 2, 2019. Retrieved from https://webcache.googleusercontent.com/search?q=cache:iH8NpWTFtgIJ:https://www.campusreform.org/%3FID%3D12053+&cd=1&hl=en&ct=clnk&gl=us.

70. Ibid.

71. Ibid.

72. H. Richard Milner IV. "Unconscious bias hurts." *Mental Health in Schools*. December 2017/January 2018. 75(4): pp. 86–87. Retrieved from http://www.ascd.org/publications/educational-leadership/dec17/vol75/num04/Unconscious-Bias-Hurts.aspx.

73. Ibid.

74. D. W. Sue, C. M. Capodilupo, G. C. Torino, et al. "Racial microaggressions in everyday life: Implications for clinical practice." *The American Psychologist*. 2007. 62(4): 271–286. See p. 271.

75. H. Richard Milner IV. "Mental health in schools." *Educational Leadership*. December 2017/January 2018. 75(4): pp. 86–87. Retrieved from http://www.ascd.org/publications/educational-leadership/dec17/vol75/num04/Unconscious-Bias-Hurts.aspx.

76. Staff. "Most important problem." *Strada-Gallup Alumni Survey*. 2018. Retrieved from https://news.gallup.com/poll/1675/most-important-problem.aspx.

77. Tyrone Howard. "How schools can foster a better racial climate." *Education Week*. May 30, 2019. Retrieved from https://www.edweek.org/ew/articles/2019/05/31/how-schools-can-foster-a-better-racial.html.

78. Ibid.

79. Susan Edelman. "Teachers allegedly told to favor black students in 'racial equity' training." *New York Post*. May 25, 2019. Retrieved from https://nypost.com/2019/05/25/teachers-allegedly-told-to-treat-black-students-as-victims-punish-whites/.

80. Ibid.

81. Ibid.

82. Ibid.

83. Ibid.

84. Ibid.

85. Sarah D. Sparks. "Students move further down school-to-prison pipeline with every school suspension." *Education Week*. July 12, 2019. Retrieved from https://blogs.edweek.org/edweek/inside-school-research/2019/07/suspension_moves_students_school_to_prison_pipeline.html.

86. Ibid.

87. Staff. "What teachers need to know about students with ODD (Oppositional Defiant Disorder)." *We Are Teachers*. April 2, 2019. Retrieved from https://www.weareteachers.com/students-with-odd/.

88. Staff. "Special education: CalEd Facts." *California Department of Education*. June 19, 2018. Retrieved from https://www.cde.ca.gov/sp/se/sr/cefspeced.asp.

89. Ibid.

90. Christina A. Samuels. "Schools' racial makeup can sway disability diagnosis." *Education Week*. June 11, 2019. Retrieved from https://www.edweek.org/ew/articles/2019/06/12/segregation-sways-disability-diagnoses.html?cmp=soc-edit-tw.

91. Ibid.

92. Laura A. Schifter, Todd Grindal, Gabriel Schwartz, et al. "Students from low-income families and special education." *The Century Foundation*. January 17, 2019. Retrieved from https://tcf.org/content/report/students-low-income-families-special-education/?agreed=1.

93. U.S. Department of Education, National Center for Education Statistics. (2019). *Digest of Education Statistics, 2017*. Chapter 2. Retrieved from https://nces.ed.gov/fastfacts/display.asp?id=64.

94. Staff. "Timeline of the Individuals with Disabilities Education Act." *University of Kansas School of Education*. April 1, 2019. Retrieved from https://educationonline.ku.edu/community/idea-timeline.

95. Mark Osborne. "Parents brawl during youth baseball game after disagreeing with 13-year-old umpire." *ABC News*. June 19, 2019. Retrieved from https://abcnews.go.com/US/parents-brawl-youth-baseball-game-disagreeing-13-year/story?id=63802898.

96. Ibid.

97. Frederick Hess. "New documents make USC look anything but innocent in varsity blues case." *Forbes*. September 9, 2019. Retrieved from https://www.forbes.com/sites/frederickhess/2019/09/09/new-documents-make-usc-look-anything-but-innocent-in-varsity-blues-case/#3afcf861248d. Cf. Julia Wick. "Newsletter: Athletic director resigns at scandal-plagued USC." *Los Angeles Times*. September 10, 2019. Retrieved from https://www.latimes.com/california/story/2019-09-10/usc-athletic-director-resigns-essential-california.

98. Julia Jones, Taylor Romine, and Evan Simko-Bednarski. "Complaint says transgender athletes in Connecticut have an unfair competitive advantage." CNN. June 20, 2019. Retrieved from https://www.cnn.com/2019/06/19/us/transgender-athletes-connecticut-education/index.html.

CHAPTER THREE

Trauma and Drama

> As a religious person, I'm worried my opinions may be suppressed in a college classroom environment. . . . I want people to understand that just because I don't agree with someone's lifestyle doesn't make my worldview less valid and it doesn't mean I don't still care about them as a person.
>
> —Anonymous university student[1]

When cultures collide at school, these collisions come from a variety of sources that exercise influence. Fellow students and peers are major influencers of contemporary and cultural practices. The smartest thing a teacher can do is to become aware of these influences and develop appropriate relationships with students in order to deter toxic and destructive practices.

Teachers should be about securing a unified and safe environment, even strategically allowing disagreements that do not affect classroom unity, classroom academics, and circumvent learning. These goals, however, may easily be made more difficult to accomplish given traumas that come to school in the lives of students. What teachers should not do is to disallow dissent by default, categorizing in advance what students can and cannot say in class.

Student Trauma

As teachers come to understand student's upbringings, they are faced with the traumas that come to school in the lives of students. Toxic experiences are embedded in the minds and hearts of many of today's students. These traumas come to school in the form of embedded hurts and pains. Some are physical, while others are emotional and psychological. In areas of high poverty, traumas may be the result of generational poverty. Along with this, additional traumas, such as sexual abuse, family drug abuse and addictions, violence, and physical abuse, are sadly all too common.

Some of America's students live each day in the midst of hyper-toxicity on the home front. In fact, their school might be the only safe place for them in today's society. To disallow their expressions is akin to the trauma they might experience at home. Therefore, it is incumbent upon all teachers to learn about their students' backgrounds and then implement strategies to build up their students' optimism and empathy in class. "Relationship-building in the classroom is essential—the one-to-one with students is indispensable—but the impact of the work is amplified and reinforced only when it occurs within the broader contexts of the school and community."[2]

Trauma is the result of something that has affected the development of trust and security in the lives of children, and data suggest that, "on average, every classroom has at least one student affected by trauma . . . [with] close to 40 percent of students in the U.S. [exposed] to some form of traumatic stressor in their lives, with sexual assault, physical assault, and witnessing domestic violence being the three most prevalent."[3]

Generational trauma is real, but it is not an absolute marker for failure in a person's life. Good teachers know this and work to alleviate as much toxicity in students' lives as possible.[4] The traumas brought to school in the lives of children are exacerbated by intergenerational issues, where similar traumas are the track record of the families from which the students emerge.

The Centers for Disease Control and Prevention state that "childhood trauma is far more pervasive than previously believed and is often invisible."[5] However, where matters can be made worse in students' lives is the assumption that a universal approach must be devised to use with all students because it must be assumed that "all children are trauma-affected and need social and emotional learning instruction and support."[6]

First, all educators must buy into the idea that there is value for them to practice social-emotional learning in their own lives. If they all do this, then they "are more likely to be passionate advocates, and the learning ecosystem is only truly healthy when all members of the community are thriving."[7]

Second, teachers should always seek to avoid known triggers for students so as not to add any semblance of trauma to their lives. Furthermore, students need activists on behalf of them as people and not so much activists for social, educational, or political causes. This includes dealing with emotionally disturbed or socially awkward students. This is one of the concerns about social-emotional learning, which is popular and becoming embedded for use in classroom curriculum and throughout school activities.

Teacher Trauma

Bullying of teachers is not a recent phenomenon. Abuse of teachers by parents, students, and administrators has been on a steep rise for at least the decades of the twenty-first century.[8] Access to more information via technology brings ease of incidental occurrence and enables their ascent in to the public domain to occur more quickly.

Bullying of teachers is sometimes accompanied by abusive behaviors. The United States is no exception when it comes to the bullying of teachers. The United States, however, does keep these events under tighter wraps than do other nations. The United Kingdom is likewise dealing with its own sets of horrific events associated with bullying and abuse of teachers. Whether it is keying of cars, physical assaults, or defiance and disrespect, parents and students are becoming more emboldened by trauma-driven anger and emotions in actual attacks upon teachers and their personal property.[9]

There is at least one point of agreement internationally in terms of why bullying is occurring more often. "Poor student behavior reflects the standards that they see at home and children cannot be held completely accountable for the values, or lack of, instilled in them at home."[10] The older the student, the more accountable he or she should be for his or her behaviors. There must be a fine line between holding students accountable and understanding the reasons behind some of the behaviors that result in negative outbursts and even violence. A lack of accountability and granting students passes on their behaviors because of their trauma is always to be the exception and not the general school or classroom policy.

Educators Traumatizing Educators

Carv Wilson, a geography teacher at Legacy Junior High in Layton, Utah,

> has seen teachers bullying each other to get their way, as well as aggressive parents who fly off the handle and threaten and intimidate their child's educators. But he says the worst case of ongoing workplace bullying he witnessed was by a principal. "I was heavily involved in school leadership both as a Davis Education Association Rep and on the school representative counsel, and I heard about or witnessed first-hand the abuse of other teachers, staff and students by this principal. . . . she specifically targeted individual teachers and

the only thing that seemed to offer any protection was membership in our local association."[11]

One thing usually not in the conversation of classroom traumas is that teachers are also victims of experiences that have left marks in their lives. Sometimes, these traumas manifest themselves and are triggered by colleagues' words or actions. The same may be true about administrators. Teacher and administrator wellness is a major concern for the newer generation of teachers and educational leaders.

In New South Wales, Australia, teachers provided details of a "toxic environment at the schools"[12] in which they worked. Complaints were lodged, and teachers were apparently bullied by an administrator into leaving the school. The toxic environment produced a "culture of fear"[13] among teachers, making them afraid to bring complaints against administrators since switching jobs would require a letter of recommendation by a "previous principal."[14] Several teachers were driven from the school by the school administrator after they lodged complaints. As a result, most teachers remained quiet and compliant out of fear or because of an inability to relinquish the effects of trauma and to move forward.

Emotional Trauma

Emotions have become the current crucible through which people define truth. Simply stated, the essence of this definition is subsumed as *the more deeply something is felt, and the longer it is felt, the truer it becomes*. But shifting emotions cannot help but lead to shifting truth. In a classroom of divergent views, each accompanied by a level of personal conviction, emotions that are perceived as truth can degenerate into an environment of unwanted toxicity.

An environment where thirty to forty children are grouped in a confined space produces an entire range of emotions on any topic. These emotions cannot all be correct expressions. Teachers deflect outbursts, help to ensure happiness, deal with student crushes, watch for student self-harm, love their students, deescalate anger, and so many other issues. Feelings, as all teachers know, are fleeting and based on whims.

One of the hazards for any classroom is the student who has endured emotional abuse at home and now brings to school with him or her an emotional imbalance through which they see the world. Likewise, what is usually missing in students from this toxic background is the ability to distinguish between negative feelings and truth. Sometimes, emotions do not make sense, but they feel good so people trust them anyway. This can lead to making poor decisions, harming others, or altering one's life.

For many reasons, the use of an emotional sense, or developing emotional intelligence—which is associated with a deep feeling and perception of something because it feels right—is not the best approach for children to determine truth. It lacks self-regulation, life experience, and facts. It also is limited by the application of a certain level of honesty with oneself. For example, if a student likes something another student posted on a popular social media page, a person can misinterpret that like and draw several conclusions. Distinguishing between experiences through emotions is difficult enough for adults to navigate, let alone children.

Teachers should encourage a balance of cognition, information, experiences, and checked emotions—especially in today's schools where emotions may very well be connected to toxic traumas in the lives of students. For further discussion, please see chapter 5.

Teaching and Schools

The culture surrounding education and the teaching profession has undergone significant changes. In some cases, it is the teachers who have changed, and their teacher-training institutions have much to do with this. In other cases, American education culture itself is supported by teacher unions and associations as well as bureaucrats reacting to the threat of lawsuits and social justice lobbyists seeking a pound of flesh for the demographic they represent.

Schools have cultures. Teaching in twenty-first-century American public schools stimulates an underlying and general unintended toxicity. The empowering of students as the center of the education universe has led to conflicts as teachers attempt to hold students accountable. Students claim to be victims of mean and uncaring teachers, leading to toxic relationships. But students are not alone. Teachers claim there are so many wedges and roadblocks to holding students accountable that they feel victimized by angry or abusive parents.

There can be no doubt that it takes strong teachers to remain focused on the priorities of academic instruction for students. American schools are more like social and political agencies today than academic institutions. This reality may elevate the social aspects of a teacher's biases while at the same time reducing emphases on academics. In elementary and junior high schools, students are being encouraged to use their educational centrism as catalysts of activism.

Such is the case with a Burlington, Vermont, high school girls' soccer team when they wore T-shirts in support of the United States Women's National Team. The T-shirts included the phrase "Equal Pay,"[15] and, because the shirts violated the soccer uniform code, the entire team was penalized for their attire. Their goal was accomplished, as the activism made national headlines.

Teachers are human and have their own personal interests. As employees, teachers must guard against their personal interests blighting the academic needs of their students. This admonition is disregarded when a teacher openly, in class, advertises association with political groups, takes on social causes for a racial or cultural demographic, or allows herself or himself to become ensconced in emotionally charged societal issues. Each of these may become toxic to those whose views are not aligned with those of the teacher, as some students would feel either compelled to agree with the teacher or be disenfranchised.

Bravery Becomes Toxic

Certain issues today should be approached cautiously and are best not to appear as drivers of a teacher's classroom instruction. Take, for example, news that appears in the headlines nearly every day. An increasing number of transgender teachers are openly sharing their coming out stories with the students.[16]

Some of these students who are the audience for their stories are in elementary grades, and their teachers do not seek parental permission to openly share their personal stories with their students.[17] Unfortunately, even the simpler events result in heated altercations at schools in most states. Just the sharing of a norm that consists of the traditional American family is enough to trigger outcries of equal access to classrooms to share alternative family stories.

There are several major cultural entities that have a hand in the changes that occur within American culture. These entities are the culture influencers and culture shapers and activist culture changers. Sometimes, cultural changes are accomplished by subtlety. Other times, the press for change is blatant. Both methods include the persistent posting of similar information on Internet newsfeeds and on websites by the hundreds of millions each day.

If something is repeated often enough and in multiple places for prolonged periods, many people tend to believe in some or all of the message that its originators meant to be conveyed. This is one reason the current generation of students have different values on a range of popular issues.[18]

Along with subtle changes, there are times when change is much more sudden and radical. In terms of politics, an example of this would be the rapid introduction and switch to the Affordable Care Act, under President Obama. Another example can be seen in education through the shifts to Common Core State Standards and then to the Every Student Succeeds Act, under Presidents Obama and Trump. President Trump's executive orders and wall building are yet other examples. Taking this to a more local level in schools means that a person or an organization given permission may present a message that agitates or offends.

Winning Can Be Toxic

There is a tendency to think that the side that wins any cultural skirmish is then somehow *on the right side of history* and holds the truth of a matter. The fact is probably all that has occurred was that one group won a lawsuit, which was decided by a judge on the merits or one with similar political and philosophical leanings. Such a mind-set toxifies an environment and tends to escalate accusations of bias. When this happens, the losing side seeks its pound of flesh, and toxicity then takes hold. Changing culture is never easy, nor should it be. When a victory is declared, sometimes Americans become more toxic, both as winners and losers. The message for teachers is for them to be on guard in terms of their personal biases toward change and, as such, also be aware of the views of those of the community in which they are employed. Educators in the middle of toxic arguments look bad to both sides.

As far as education and schooling are concerned, teachers and parents have disagreed and even battled over issues in the past and will continue to do so into the future. The reason toxic issues can be expected to become sources of rage to some groups is that each was placed on the radar for policy reform by politicians, bureaucrats, teachers' unions, and social justice organizations. The issues were forced upon people and not derived by sensible conversations and consent of the majority of constituents. The following are hot-button issues for today's public schools, and teachers should take extra care when addressing them: (1) race, (2) religion, (3) family background, (4) gender, (5) culture, (6) sexual orientation, and (7) learning styles.[19]

Substances Are Toxic
This book is primarily about the toxicity in schools surrounding personalities, teachings, and culture in general in America. However, any book on detoxing American public schools that did not address the other national

epidemic facing the nation would be missing an opportunity to present information for the reader.

The fact is incontrovertible: Americans are addicts. The United States has serious addiction problems, and these addictions include marijuana, heroin, alcohol, vaping, pornography, violence, and the list goes on. Specifically, America is overrun with legal and prescription drugs and various other illegal substances. In order to completely detox our nation's youth from substances, it would require more than Herculean effort—it would require a miracle. That being stated, America is not alone in dealing with addiction.

The following data are examples of the enormity of the ever-growing problems with addictions in the United States. These addictions do not escape the nation's children and youth. Whether children are drug babies, traumatized by parents with addictions, or addicts themselves, our nation's schools deal with what President Trump has declared a "national public health emergency."[20]

Drugs

Data from the Pew Research Center indicate that "Americans overwhelmingly see drug addiction as a problem in their local community, regardless of whether they live in an urban, suburban or rural area."[21] There are an estimated one in seven Americans who are drug abusers or addicted to drugs. "Nine-in-ten Americans who live in a rural area say drug addiction is either a major or minor problem in their community, as do 87% in urban and 86% in suburban areas."[22] Along with alcohol, there have been "significant increases . . . across the country. This abuse has significantly impacted K–12 school-age students as well as those pursuing postsecondary education."[23] In 2016 alone, "63,600 people died of a drug overdose. . . . Opioids—ranging from illegal street drugs like heroin to prescription painkillers—have played an especially lethal role."[24]

In terms of the opioid epidemic, it reaches down into elementary schools. In that light, according to the US Department of Education, the following are some warning signs for the possibilities that students might be impacted by opioids, alcohol, or another addictive substance. To be fair, some students may exhibit one or more of these behaviors but not have a problem with addiction.

Elementary School Students[25]
- Poor mental and/or motor development
- Memory and perception problems
- Speech and language problems

- Developmental delays
- Reduced decision-making abilities
- Impaired self-regulation
- Poor response to stressful situations

Middle School Students[26]
- Anxiety
- Depression
- Secretive behaviors
- Poor hygiene and/or changes in physical appearance
- Disruptive behavior
- Rapid changes in mood
- Decline in academic performance or attendance

High School Students[27]
- Mood or personality changes
- Depression
- Hyperactivity
- Health and hygiene issues
- Changes in relationships with friends and family
- Problems with police
- Unhealthy peer and/or dating relationships
- Disengagement from school
- Poor attendance or dropping out

States that are passing recreational marijuana laws are not helping much with the drug epidemic. DUIs are up, students are evidencing cognitive issues in classes, and addiction to a cannabis that is engineered to be much more potent than the marijuana from previous decades is one of the reasons. While it is important to note that marijuana remains an illegal Schedule-1 drug,[28] the following geographic reality has implications far beyond the law. "Thirty-three states and the District of Columbia currently have passed laws broadly legalizing marijuana in some form."[29]

On a national level, the drug epidemic is too large to handle. On local levels, there are some strategies to assist and cause incremental changes in support of our students and their families. To begin, school districts and local health agencies have literature and other resources available to help. This epidemic will have to be solved one person at a time and on a local level. However, larger communities have to have the will to drive the solutions forward.

Parents who suspect that their child has a problem with drugs or alcohol should contact the school counselors and request support. They can also call their clergy or local health departments for advice. Each student is different, and the strategies to assist may be adjusted to fit the needs of the family and student.

Next, parents would benefit greatly by deepening their relationships with their children, making certain to let them know they are loved unconditionally, regardless of the problems they are facing. Facing the issue as a family unit will strengthen the bond between parents and children.

In addition, parents should do two things to enhance their information on the issues facing their children today. First, they should know who their children's friends are and what they are talking about in text messages and on their social media pages as well as in private video chats and online photo posts. Holding children accountable from the very beginning with smart technology is smart parenting. Loving them without judgment is even smarter.

Lastly, parents must become informed of the temptations and dangers that face their children each day. Getting to know about the issues in society, the cultural icons admired by their children, and the entertainment that fills their minds means taking the time to delve into their world.

Parents will be amazed at what is out there tempting their children. But they should never be surprised by this. Culture changes and people invent new dangers. Table 3.1 includes addictions that make their ways into classrooms all across America.[30]

Any one or a number of issues described above could pop up on any given day in the life of a child. The residuals can be found at schools every day. The fact is that, along with drug and alcohol addiction, our students are ensnared by other addictions. The problems can seem overwhelming for parents.

Concerned parents could start a support group with others who are dealing with similar issues. This is a great way to share concerns and offer assistance and emotional support as well as stay abreast of current culture. This way, when those difficult conversations occur with children—and they will occur—parents can be informed and rational and, most of all, understanding.

A Revolution in the Making?

Sustained cultural changes that have taken decades to accomplish are no longer the focus among modern culture shapers and activists. Revolutions are the new standard rally cry. Talking heads on cable networks and click bait Internet purveyors are aplenty, thus spinning issues in ways they hope to affect their audience and sway opinion.

Table 3.1. Addictions in American Society

Substance Abused or Addiction	Facts
Drugs	1 in 7 people in the United States will face substance addiction. Opioids such as heroin are at epidemic levels.
Alcohol	70% of teens have consumed at least one alcoholic beverage by the time they reach 18. Children as young as age 12 have been diagnosed as alcoholic. More than 90% of underage drinking is related to binge drinking.
Vaping	Highly addictive nicotine levels exist in some products. The American Medical Association is urging Americans to stop vaping until they can determine what exactly is causing vaping-related illnesses and lung issues. More than 3 million US high school students used e-cigarettes in 2018, a 78% increase in use.
Pornography	12 percent of all Internet websites are pornographic. 25 percent of all online search engine requests are related to sex. 68 million requests for pornography per day. 35 percent of all Internet downloads are pornographic. 40 million Americans are regular visitors to porn sites. 70 percent of men aged 18 to 24 visit a porn site at least once per month. The average age of first exposure to Internet porn is 11. The largest consumer group of Internet porn is men aged 35 to 49. One-third of all Internet porn users are female. The most popular day of the week for watching porn is Sunday. The most popular day of the year for watching porn is Thanksgiving
Smart Devices	Nearly 50% of parents stated their children were addicted to smart technology and screen time. Over one-third of parents said the same thing about themselves. Nearly 93% of 6–12 year old children have access to smart phones or tablets for hours each day, and nearly 70% of these same children have their own personal devices.

Particularly vulnerable is the age demographic of early teenagers through the mid-20s, which is essentially Generation Z.[31] This range of young people is the easiest to influence emotionally, as they are in the process of forming personal opinions and seek to be the first of their group to have access to new and exciting experiences.

Americans are on edge, and factions are gaining more and more power. Time will tell where the soon-to-be largest generation will come down on issues. America seems primed for a cultural revolution, which probably will not be a peaceful one.

Drama in American Culture

There is no particular form or fashion by which a list of toxic teachings or beliefs can be 100 percent causatively connected to negative effects on American culture. Regardless, toxicity is often the result of reactions to changes that usually marginalize and emphasize differences to the exclusion of beliefs and practices of others.

Whether culture is changed from decisions handed down from liberal or conservative courts, following the personal philosophies or practices of elites, change does not please everyone. For some people, change is enough for the production of a lethal educational environment, even if a decision is handed down through the constitutionally created Supreme Court.

Court Decision Drama

The American court system has enormously impacted the lives of all people living in the United States. Some of the decisions handed down by the courts have changed American culture dramatically. Depending on which presidential administration has been able to appoint justices and which political group has been able to confirm these justices, the Supreme Court's decisions are sometimes viewed as partisan. Its decisions can change American culture by appearing to legislate from the bench or interpret the Constitution in a much more literalist fashion. Everyone understands the SCOTUS is the court of last resort on constitutional issues.

Social activists understand how to use the courts to achieve their goals. Whether the issue is immigration, same-sex marriage, abortion, restroom use, transgendered competitors, prayer in schools, or the right to wear certain hats or politically messaged clothing, courts are usually the ultimate in deciding cultural and social issues. Other than that, people are left to decide whether or not to adhere to the changes that conflict with their beliefs or to violate new precedents established by the courts.

Activists for both conservative and liberal causes use the courts to their advantage. Court decisions play large roles in fueling some of the toxicity manifesting itself in American schools.

Therefore, when asking how and why culture changes, and whether these changes lead to a toxic culture, one of the first places to look for an answer is the American court system. For example, when the Supreme Court decided that reading a daily passage from the Bible over the intercom at schools violated students' rights, the uproar was intense.

When a student's famous atheist mother, Madeline Murray O'Hair, sued to have corporate school prayer ended, the environment in public schools was affected. Prayer was toxic to atheists, and then removal of prayer became toxic to those who prayed.

Trauma is induced in culture with each controversial Supreme Court decision. Decisions about education have national implications, and schools then must comply. This is how culture changes, both for the victors and for the defeated. Even appointing and confirming a justice to the Court has become highly toxic. From Bork to Thomas to Kavanaugh, Americans were agitated as they watched the toxic environment created by political partisans.

Elitist Drama
There are people in culture who command media attention by their mere presence. These people are usually placed by others in categories of society under the term *elites*. The elites of society usually refers to those with many resources, including money, fame, influence, and power. Members of Hollywood-type professions and social status, politicians, athletes, and entertainers qualify as elites.

In addition, elites are always in the spotlight, and their words and actions are broadcast with some measure of importance for everyone else. The cultural impact of elites upon millions of people is astounding. Their opinions are often heard first, and their words and actions are often progressive on social and political issues.

Everything from phrases used, to clothing worn, to political and social beliefs and sexual practices is often channeled through one or more of these elites with the sole purpose to influence culture. For example, if a family rises to the top in America for their clothing line, their elite status affords them attention. If a person has a sexual experience and releases a homemade sex tape, their status rises in the media.

Elites wearing their clothes enables their brand to be seen by millions, which is how cultural fads begin. Their words and phrases are often added to the English lexicon as urban catchphrases. Likewise, now that F-bombs are acceptable as adjectives and adverbs, the acceptability had to begin somewhere. Cultural toxicity usually follows cultural coarseness. One needs to look no further than elites for an impact on language coarseness. If anyone wonders how coarse language changes over time, all a person has to do is check the influencers in a person's life. People do learn from others.

Is there any doubt when elites claim something about sexuality or gender, or masculinity or race, followers begin adopting both their rhetoric and their practice? If a lifestyle is accepted by someone popular, then others sense acceptability. Did the nation not experience this change with the Clinton impeachment of the 1990s? Parents had to explain to their children why oral sex was sex.

The power of elites over culture is real. The Internet and social media are the conduits of influence for the elites. Their drama is their follower's drama, especially as it influences the younger generation seeking an identity of its own.

An extreme example of how elites can affect the pulse of a generation is the hatred directed at President Trump. Some Hollywood elites have referred to President Trump as Hitler and as a Nazi. Others have called for his assassination and that all of the people who either voted for him or are his followers are white nationalists and racists. These statements are emphasized and even embellished by various media outlets; before long, groups are at odds with each other, and a dangerous toxicity results. Once established, this toxicity makes its way very rapidly across college campuses and into K–12 classrooms.

Higher Education Drama
Some professors in higher education institutions employ conscious efforts into shaping American culture. In some cases, depending on the institution, national notoriety is expected for their work. The platform for communicating one's stance on an issue takes center stage and makes the institution look good to those with agreeable positions. It also brings in funding. Hillsdale College, Liberty University, and Claremont Colleges are good examples.

Institutions of higher learning are supposed to be places where students can receive well-rounded educations and be prepared for gainful employment. In far too many universities and colleges, there are obvious biases and political leanings that today are intolerable of any positions favoring one side or another.

Most would agree that certain departments at college lean toward the progressive left politically. The inability to tolerate dissent has become a hallmark of higher learning environments, and institutions that allow this toxic environment to flourish are actually factories producing *disciples of dissent*. Such places are encampments, entrenched in firm beliefs and guardians of the status quo for their constituents and their donors.

Race and Nationalism
The following example is an illustration of some of the toxic racial rhetoric that is allowed to occur on college campuses. At the University of Georgia,

some alumni "say they will not donate to the school again after administrators didn't take any disciplinary action against a teaching assistant who made controversial comments such as 'some white people may have to die for black communities to be made whole in this struggle to advance freedom.'"[32] Irami Osei-Frimpong, "a UGA teaching assistant . . . previously made comments such as . . . 'fighting white people is a skill.' The TA was accused of intentionally omitting a 2011 trespassing arrest from his admission application and not disclosing his attendance at the University of Chicago, which led to a university investigation."[33]

Another example illustrates the impunity with which some professors are able to expound hateful rhetoric. Professor Reza Aslan (University of California, Riverside) posted his anti-Trump vitriol on Twitter: "After today there is no longer any room for nuance. The President is a white nationalist terror leader. His supporters—ALL OF THEM—are by definition white nationalist terror supporters. The MAGA hat is a KKK hood. And this evil racist scourge must be eradicated from society."[34] In a follow-up comment posted to one of the president's senior counselors, the professor seemed to threaten her life when he wrote, "We are all so f***ing fed up with you racist GOPers and your bad faith bulls***. . . . You are the 'depraved evil' we need to eradicate."[35]

Over fifty million students attend K–12 schools, and millions more are in colleges and universities, from part-time to full-time, including both online and face-to-face. The addition of reputations of teachers and faculty associations, their political positions, and their voting bloc is assumed.

Today, the concerns are great for people of all political persuasions. Racial divisions seem to have deepened since 2010. As an example, "after the November 2016 elections, colleges saw a widely reported spike in white supremacist flier-posting and hate-inspired incidents. . . . White-supremacist groups like Identity Europa, Patriot Front, and Vanguard America are some of the more notable that are taking aim at colleges."[36]

The racial toxicity on some college campuses is growing, and the marginalization of races continues to increase. As colleges move to ban one group's expression based on race, such a ban becomes toxic to other groups. However, in not banning any toxic racial expression, toxicity continues to grow unabated. Colleges are in a quandary, but this is not the only social issue facing them in the twenty-first century.

LGBTQ+ and Christian Colleges
As a compromise, some Christian colleges and universities allow LGBTQ+ groups organizational recognition on campus in efforts to practice inclusion over doctrine. Calvin College, Campbell University, Eastern Mennonite

University, and Fuller Theological Seminary are examples of some of the "approximately 40–45 LGBTQ student groups at evangelical universities across the U.S."[37]

As a sobering reminder over toxicity in the past over race, Jonathan Parks-Ramage warns Christian institutions of higher education:

> Even Christian universities that don't receive federal funding could eventually lose their tax-exempt status over LGBTQ discrimination. Many leaders cite the 1983 Supreme Court ruling in *Bob Jones University v. United States*—where a university was denied tax-exempt status because of its discriminatory policy against interracial dating—as a precedent-setting case that could dramatically impact Christian universities. . . . [According to Carl Trueman] "In an era where a close analogy is assumed between civil rights regarding race and civil rights regarding sexual identity, the Bob Jones precedent could easily lead to the revocation of tax-exempt status for schools committed to traditional views of marriage and sexual morality." Though it could take decades, civil rights progress for the LGBTQ community "is likely to annihilate many of those institutions which refuse to accommodate themselves to the dominant sexual culture."
>
> But as many conservative religious administrators prepare to fight to the death to discriminate against LGBTQ students—some going so far as to sign the anti-LGBTQ Nashville Statement—another crucial question arises: Who are they fighting for? Fifty-three percent of young evangelicals support same-sex marriage, and students on conservative Christian campuses are becoming increasingly welcoming of their LGBTQ peers. Even if certain schools maintain their policies, how many applicants will be interested in attending a college that denies certain students basic civil rights?[38]

Christian institutions are either going to have to change their policies in the near future or face consequences. In the minds of some, these consequences will be much greater than the consequences of reducing adherence to a biblical teaching on homosexuality and same-sex marriage. To advocates of orthodox Christian beliefs, they view this government denigrating the freedom of religion under the First Amendment. Like abortion and race, it is nearly impossible to find a middle ground with issues that present themselves as inherently toxic.

Social Organizations Drama
The formation of family values is an important factor in child development. Children need stability and should be able to trust what they learn at home is of great value to their growth and upbringing. However, far too many American families are now relying on schools, churches, and other social agencies

to assist them in rearing their children. Certain demographic groups are suffering from a lack of two-parent homes and are absent the balance necessary for well-rounded upbringings.

Organizations and social agencies step in to assist as they can to fill these gaps in children's lives, and schools serve in a primary role as gap fillers. A culture that supports single parents is admirable. But the culture that enables such families generationally has already affected children of those families with social fabric trauma. This trauma is often cyclical and becomes a dramatic toxin to communities as it plays out in the very schools meant to assist those communities.[39]

Social institutions as a broad category is meant to encompass organized entities that have roles in the lives of people and provide either direct access to community or vicarious opportunities to impact communities on a more local level. Churches are a good example of these institutions, as they have doctrinal tenets, expectations, and even codes of behaviors for their members. Beliefs run the gamut in terms of social involvement in culture. For example, certain denominations are struggling over what to do with ordination of previously atypical groups or their decades-to-centuries-old teachings against various sexual practices and alternative definitions of marriage.

What organizations and schools must understand is that their efforts to deal with student trauma must not re-traumatize students by establishing toxic environments. Children are traumatized as a result of very different experiences. Individual student trauma "is best understood as the result of an event, series of events, or set of circumstances that is experienced by an individual as physically or emotionally harmful or life threatening and that has lasting effects."[40]

Schools and other organizations that claim to focus on trauma-informed practice in their classrooms or business comprehend the three-Rs of trauma-informed care. These are summarized in the realization of "the widespread impact of trauma"[41] and that in many people's lives there are avenues of recovery available. They also include a recognition of "signs and symptoms of trauma"[42] as well as incorporate "knowledge about trauma into policies, procedures, and practices."[43] But what happens when families are traumatized by an organization's beliefs and practices or their schools consenting to new cultural paradigms that counter families' values?

On February 8, 1910, the Boy Scouts of America was formed. A recent change to the charter of the organization meant that the social institution is now culturally referred to as scouting, where any gender is now welcome to join. Previously designated by the terms *boys* and *girls*, the Boy Scouts was considered exclusive and uninviting.

Changes such as these, on the one hand, have opened doors in the name of equity to counter "sexism." On the other hand, such changes are not completely understood and are deemed punitive to boys. Either way, changes such as these result in toxicity on one or more levels. Take, for example, a young Muslim in Scout troops. Their religious culture would not allow females into the mix with boys because of the fundamental injunctions of mixing of the genders.

Should any special exceptions be made for Muslims having only boys in their troops? This becomes even more a concern when a youth seeks transgender reassignment or does not desire to become Muslim, but wishes to join a Muslim boys' troop to be with friends.[44] What is toxic to some is not toxic to all, but toxicity affects all involved on some level.

The cultural spillover from families and social institutions finds its way into schools and becomes a source of toxicity. In fact, the cultural impact that some professional institutions possess over education policy is in itself toxic at times. In other instances, going against the professional consensus is toxic. For example, some "psychologists are scared to question transgender ideology," and medical general practitioners questioning the trend "are afraid of being branded transphobic." Meanwhile, "teens are being wrongly diagnosed."[45] Conclusions like these in a profession that has adopted a progressive ideology is not welcome and is often career ending.[46] When standing up for truth in science becomes toxic, who then can be trusted?

Activism Drama
Activism on the part of a teacher who decides to go it alone on an issue can bring serious drama to the school. Activism and advocacy for social causes have their places, but teachers should question whether America's K–12 schools are the cultural breeding ground for such activities. Informing students about academic content is one thing. Conversely, some perceive teachers who practice an activism for social causes as a form of personal indoctrination. Others see it as a grooming tool for recruitment toward a perspective that may conflict with home. Each approach brings with it a natural toxicity.

Children should not be subjected to a teacher's personal agenda in ways that influence their thinking—especially absent any significant academic connection. Teachers must not evangelize students or inform them about personal issues that are considered toxic to the community at large. Any disregard can be construed as not caring about the values of the majority of families in the school district. Unfortunately, the self has become the object of celebration in this toxic era of identity politics. One's self-proclamations are more toxic today as individuals usurp the corporate conscience of the masses.

Certainly, teachers can respond to questions students ask them. Still, when teachers are motivated to expose students to an alternate culture involving anything to do with issues that are highly controversial, if not inflammatory—with the intent to drive home a point about rights—teachers create an emotional environment of conflict.

An example of such activism that became toxic and caused an uproar is the story about a biological man desiring to become a surgical woman. He took it upon himself to explain what he was going through in the transition process and showed a film about transgenderism. He also taught students politically correct pronouns to use in everyday language in order to address a host of additional genders that have been added to society's litany. The teacher did all of these things without prior consent of the administration and the parents.

One of the consequences of a toxic classroom is the inability to trust the teacher. In this case, the teacher violated the trust he was given by parents and employer. In his defense, the teacher thought his personal drama with his identity would help students who were also struggling with their identity. The major difference is that children do not struggle over things in ways that adults struggle with them. Assuming they do is misguided.[47]

Ideological Drama
Change is accepted very differently by the very society expected to change. Acceptance of change is seldom based on one factor alone. Emotions, vested personal or financial interests, politics, status quo, and morality are a few factors to consider when figuring the extent of societal change. Progressives are more inclined to seek progress at the risk of offending the majority. Conversely, traditionalists want change as well, usually at the expense of the minority as they would seek to reverse some of the progressives' changes.

Traditionalists are not in favor of widespread, rapid change. Traditionalists are intent on passing on knowledge and experiences they have from their lives to their own children. For example, to the traditionalist, school holds some special meaning. It was meant as a place of learning and interaction between boys and girls. It was not a place of social engineering or altering norms, even though many questioned schooling during the Cold War conflict and Vietnam War. That being said, the baby boomer generation might view the *ducking and covering drills* and the pressure of learning *math and science* during the Cold War period with the former Soviet Union less glibly than others.

Progressives have a different take on school. They maintain that school is a harbinger for change and that teachers are to act as change agents.

Progressives also favor exposing children to the newest ideas in culture and that society has a responsibility to support schools to be these places of change. Teachers can hardly catch their breath before another change comes down the line from the state level.

Not all educational change used to be toxic. But something is vastly different about the changes in America's public schools today. The academic urgency has given way to social urgency. The conditions of students are overwhelming the system. The pendulum has definitely swung from high-stakes, mind-numbing assessments to making certain students feel socially and emotionally well in their daily lives.

What is most interesting about all of the changes that occur in schools is that teachers are choosing to leave the profession earlier than in years past. Whether they are progressives or traditionalists, toxic school environments play a role as to whether some teachers will or will not continue in their careers.

When it comes to changes in culture, James Madison understood the delicate balance between factions and the common good of the majority. His warning still speaks volumes today. Madison wrote:

> It is in vain to say that enlightened statesmen will be able to adjust these clashing interests, and render them all subservient to the public good. Enlightened statesmen will not always be at the helm. Nor, in many cases, can such an adjustment be made at all without taking into view indirect and remote considerations, which will rarely prevail over the immediate interest which one party may find in disregarding the rights of another or the good of the whole.[48]

Politically Correct Drama

Political correctness has different meanings to different groups. To some, the phrase implies limiting words and placing restrictions on speech that a few dislike. To others, political correctness is holding the beliefs of a progressive culture and advancing an agenda to change the social and moral climates of the nation.

One of the results of political correctness is the notion that people should be protected from anything offensive. Groups have established spaces to shield students from anything that would cause emotional upset or distress or come across as challenging. In one sense, political correctness is a tool to avoid toxicity for a generation whose beliefs and practices are just as toxic.

When discussing political correctness, there is a squishy center that is difficult to grasp. This is illustrated by Jonny Thakkar with his statement that "a lot depends on what we mean by political correctness. (Jonathan)

. . . Chait thinks of it as a whole 'style of politics' that is intolerant of dissent and obsessed with identity. That analysis packs in too much, threatening to turn political correctness into a floating signifier whose real referent is 'stuff that annoys me.'"[49]

Thakkar continues and suggests that the practical application of political correctness results in "the practice of regulating our speech in light of political ideals and values."[50]

What remains toxic about political correctness to this day is "those who claim to have been silenced by political correctness typically have the legal right to say whatever it is they claim they cannot say. What they are really objecting to is the social pressure not to make use of that formal freedom—a pressure that, they argue, reduces their real freedom to express themselves."[51] However, the reality is that "real freedom of speech is always limited to some degree. Outside of therapy, there are no secure contexts in which adults have the absolute right to speak whatever issues they have on their minds—and do with impunity."[52]

The toxic nature of political correctness arises when one political group decides that another political group should be silenced for its disagreements.[53] For example, nearly three-fourths of college students desire their campus and professors to be inclined toward being open to hearing dissenting views.[54] But this is not reality. A recent Gallup poll indicated that about two-thirds of recent college graduates did not "strongly agree with the statement that they were comfortable in voicing minority opinions in class."[55] Student apprehension on college campuses remains pervasive. The Knight Foundation reported in *College Pulse*[56] that "more than two thirds of U.S. college students said that their college campus environments prevent people from expressing beliefs due to the possibility of seeming offensive."[57]

Most teachers did not sign up to teach with the ultimate goal of shaping society in general. They did not sign up to be activists for the agenda of a small percentage of fringe groups in society. When focusing on education becomes toxic and extreme, American schools will have become social agencies with academics as an afterthought. The unfortunate truth is that American schools are already on their way toward this reality and nothing short of a major detox can affect the outcome.

Notes

1. Ethan Cai. "Most college grads say campus climate prevents them from expressing beliefs." *Campus Reform*. June 18, 2019. Retrieved from https://www.campusreform.org/?ID=13345.

2. Alex Shevrin Venet. "The how and why of trauma-informed teaching." *Edutopia*. August 3, 2018. Retrieved from https://www.edutopia.org/article/how-and-why-trauma-informed-teaching.

3. Lea Waters and Tom Brunzell. "Five ways to support students affected by trauma." *Greater Good Magazine*. August 13, 2018. Retrieved from https://greatergood.berkeley.edu/article/item/five_ways_to_support_students_affected_by_trauma.

4. Joyce Dorado and Vicki Zakrzewski. "How to help a traumatized child in the classroom." *Greater Good Magazine*. October 23, 2013. Retrieved from https://greatergood.berkeley.edu/article/item/the_silent_epidemic_in_our_classrooms.

5. Alex Shevrin Venet. "The how and why of trauma-informed teaching."

6. Ibid.

7. Ibid.

8. Anthea Lipsett. "Abuse of teachers by parents and pupils on the rise, says survey." *The Guardian*. April 6, 2009. Retrieved from https://www.theguardian.com/education/2009/apr/06/teachers-abuse-violence-pupils-parents.

9. Ibid.

10. Ibid.

11. Cindy Long. "Bullying of teachers pervasive in many schools." *NEA Today*. May 16, 2012. Retrieved from http://neatoday.org/2012/05/16/bullying-of-teachers-pervasive-in-many-schools-2/.

12. Charis Chang. "Claims of 'culture of fear' in schools as bullying allegations emerge." *News.com.au*. September 7, 2018. Retrieved from https://www.news.com.au/lifestyle/parenting/school-life/claims-of-culture-of-fear-in-schools-as-bullying-allegations-emerge/news-story/c584e7c816d4482cdae97e6d75bffa6a.

13. Ibid.

14. Ibid.

15. Alaa Elassar. "A girls soccer team was penalized for their 'equal pay' shirts. Now their message is being celebrated." *CNN*. October 21, 2019. Retrieved from https://www.cnn.com/2019/10/21/us/burlington-girls-soccer-equal-pay-trnd/index.html.

16. Meera Jagannathan. "Five brave LGBTQ teachers tell Moneyish how they came out to the students." *Market Watch*. June 8, 2018. Retrieved from https://www.marketwatch.com/story/five-brave-lgbtq-teachers-tell-moneyish-how-they-came-out-to-their-students-2018-06-08.

17. Video. "Wisconsin elementary school 'teacher's transgender coming out' video outrages parents." *Yahoo News*. June 4, 2019. Retrieved from https://www.yahoo.com/news/wisconsin-elementary-school-teachers-transgender-210639365.html.

18. Susan Miller. "The young are regarded as the most tolerant generation. That's why results of this LGBTQ survey are 'alarming.'" *USA Today*. June 24, 2019. Retrieved from https://www.usatoday.com/story/news/nation/2019/06/24/lgbtq-acceptance-millennials-decline-glaad-survey/1503758001/. Cf. "GLAAD survey: Young people become less accepting of LGBTQ people because of Trump and 'newness' factor." *The Daily Beast*. June 24, 2019. Retrieved from https://www.the

dailybeast.com/glaad-survey-young-people-become-less-accepting-of-lgbtq-people-because-of-trump-and-newness-factor?ref=scroll.

19. Michael Dimock. "How America changed during Barack Obama's presidency." Pew Research Center. January 10, 2017. Retrieved from https://www.pewresearch.org/2017/01/10/how-america-changed-during-barack-obamas-presidency/.

20. Dan Merica. "Trump declares opioid epidemic a national public health emergency." *CNN.* October 26, 2017. Retrieved from https://www.cnn.com/2017/10/26/politics/donald-trump-opioid-epidemic/index.html.

21. John Gramlich. "As fatal overdoses rise, many Americans see drug addiction as a major problem in their community." Pew Research Center. May 30, 2018. Retrieved from https://www.pewresearch.org/fact-tank/2018/05/30/as-fatal-overdoses-rise-many-americans-see-drug-addiction-as-a-major-problem-in-their-community/.

22. Ibid.

23. Staff. "Combating substance abuse in schools." *Homeroom.* January 17, 2019. Retrieved from https://blog.ed.gov/2019/01/how-to-identify-and-support-students-suffering-from-substance-abuse/.

24. John Gramlich. "As fatal overdoses rise, many Americans see drug addiction as a major problem in their community."

25. Staff. "Combating substance abuse in schools."

26. Ibid.

27. Ibid.

28. Staff. "Drug scheduling." *United States Drug Enforcement Agency.* 2019. Retrieved from https://www.dea.gov/drug-scheduling.

29. Staff. "State marijuana laws in 2019 map." *Governing the States and Localities.* 2019. Retrieved from https://www.governing.com/gov-data/safety-justice/state-marijuana-laws-map-medical-recreational.html.

30. Josh Hafner. Drugs. "Surgeon General: 1 in 7 in USA will face substance addiction." *USA Today.* November 17, 2016. Retrieved from https://www.usatoday.com/story/news/nation-now/2016/11/17/surgeon-general-1-7-us-face-substance-addiction/93993474/. Cf. Staff. Alcohol. "Underage drinking statistics with the U.S." *Alcohol.org.* July 5, 2019. Retrieved from https://www.alcohol.org/teens/underage-drinking-stats/. Gabriella Borter and Matthew Lavietes. Vaping. "From removing doors to checking sleeves, U.S. schools seek to snuff out vaping." Reuters. September 11, 2019. Retrieved from https://www.reuters.com/article/us-health-vaping/from-removing-doors-to-checking-sleeves-u-s-schools-seek-to-snuff-out-vaping-idUSKCN1VW17G; Robert Weiss. Pornography. "The prevalence of porn." *Psych Central.* March 2019. Retrieved from https://blogs.psychcentral.com/sex/2013/05/the-prevalence-of-porn/; Marilyn Wedge. Smart Devices. "Is your child addicted to mobile devices?" *Psychology Today.* March 6, 2018. Retrieved from https://www.psychologytoday.com/us/blog/suffer-the-children/201803/is-your-child-addicted-mobile-devices.

31. Ernest J. Zarra III. *The entitled generation: Helping teachers teach and reach the minds and hearts of Generation Z.* Lanham, Maryland: Rowman & Littlefield Publishers.

32. Adam Sabes. "Exclusive: UGA loses donations, possibly tuition money, over TA remarks." *Campus Reform*. May 13, 2019. Retrieved from https://www.campusreform.org/?ID=12221.

33. Ibid.

34. Ethan Cai. "Calif. prof: Trump supporters are 'white nationalist terror supporters.'—ALL OF THEM." *Campus Reform*. August 5, 2019. Retrieved from https://wwwt2.campusreform.org/?ID=13533.

35. Ibid.

36. Emma Kerr. "White supremacists are targeting college campuses like never before." *The Chronicle of Higher Education*. February 1, 2018. Retrieved from https://www.chronicle.com/article/White-Supremacists-Are/242403. Cf. "Stephen C. Finley, Biko M. Gray, and Lori Latrice Martin. "Affirming our values: African American scholars, white virtual mobs, and the complicity of white university administrators." *American Association of University Professors Journal of Academic Freedom*. Volume 9, pp. 1–20.

37. Jonathan Parks-Ramage. "The queer movement changing hearts on Christian campuses." *Medium*. September 19, 2018. Retrieved from https://medium.com/s/youthnow/apu-calvin-college-intervarsity-activism-queer-movement-changing-hearts-on-christian-campuses-ccbeb0844cdf.

38. Ibid.

39. Carrie Gaffney. "When schools cause trauma." *Teaching Tolerance*. Summer 2019. Issue 62. Retrieved from https://www.tolerance.org/magazine/summer-2019/when-schools-cause-trauma.

40. Ibid.

41. Ibid.

42. Ibid.

43. Ibid.

44. Nathan Greenberg. "Why I still won't put my son in the Boy Scouts." *Huffington Post*. December 7, 2019. Retrieved from https://www.huffpost.com/entry/why-i-still-wont-put-my-s_b_7963582. Cf. Staff. "NJ: Two traditions inspire faithful scouts." *Council on American-Islamic Relations*. November 28, 2007. Retrieved from https://www.cair.com/nj_two_traditions_inspire_faithful_scouts.

45. Sanchez Manning. "Experts reveal psychologists are scared to question transgender ideology." *Daily Mail*. July 14, 2019. Retrieved from https://www.dailymail.co.uk/news/article-7244783/Academics-medical-experts-fears-children-number-seeking-sex-change-operations-sky-rockets.html. Cf. Heather Bruskell-Evans and Michelle Moore. *Inventing transgender children and young people*. 2019. Cambridge, England: Cambridge Scholars Publishing.

46. Matt Slick. "Examples of persecution of people who do not agree with homosexuality." *Christian Apologetics and Research Ministry*. n.d. Retrieved from https://carm.org/homosexual-persecution-of-christians.

47. Video. "Wisconsin elementary school teacher's 'transgender coming out' video outrages parents." *Yahoo News*. Retrieved from https://ca.news.yahoo.com/wisconsin-elementary-school-teachers-transgender-210639365.html.

48. James Madison. "The Federalist No. 10: The utility of the union as a safeguard against domestic faction and insurrection." *Daily Advertiser*. November 22, 1787. Retrieved from https://www.constitution.org/fed/federa10.htm.

49. Jonny Thakkar. "Putting the political back in politically correct." *The Chronicle of Higher Education*. June 12, 2019. Retrieved from https://www.chronicle.com/article/Putting-the-Political-Back-in/246476.

50. Ibid.

51. Ibid.

52. Ibid.

53. Ibid.

54. Ethan Cai. "Most college grads say campus climate prevents them from expressing beliefs."

55. Ibid.

56. Knight Foundation. "Free expression on college campuses." *College Pulse*. Retrieved from https://kf-site-production.s3.amazonaws.com/media_elements/files/000/000/351/original/Knight-CP-Report-FINAL.pdf.

57. Ethan Cai. "Most college grads say campus climate prevents them from expressing beliefs."

CHAPTER FOUR

Are You a Toxic Teacher?

> The influence of factious leaders may kindle a flame . . . but will be unable to spread a general conflagration. . . . A religious sect may degenerate into a political faction . . . but the variety of sects dispersed over the entire face of it must secure the national councils against any danger from that source.
>
> —James Madison[1]

When researching toxicity in public schools, any discussion must take into account a host of factors, each of which is of great importance. Students are affected by a number of influences that factor into their lives. These influences include parents, students, politics, administrators, and even school environments. But there is one major factor that tends to outweigh the others, that is, the impact of a teacher on the lives of students. If a teacher is toxic, then the effects on students have long-term implications.

This chapter is meant for teachers to examine themselves, their actions and words, and to examine instructional methods and styles of teaching as a matter of self-reflection. As teachers look inward, each has to realize there is no one identifier of what it means to be toxic. So, for example, when parents say there is a toxic classroom on their child's school campus, this statement can pertain to one of three general ideas: (1) the physical environment is causing illness, (2) students and parents are causing extreme stress levels, or (3) the teacher or administrator is causing a toxic environment for students and colleagues.

The fact that the classroom teacher is the overseer of most things that arise within the context of a school environment means teachers might be viewed as ground zero for toxicity. Certainly, a combination effect of the three elements above can lay the groundwork for potential negation to the longevity of a teacher's career. The negation of a teacher's career can also negatively impact student learning and the emotional makeup of the class as a whole.

Toxic teachers are not necessarily bad teachers. The fact that a teacher may not be liked as a colleague does not qualify a teacher as being toxic. Those who are doing the disliking may well be the toxic ones.

There is something similar about being both in front of the classroom and behind the steering wheel of a car. Most would argue that it comes down to power. So, without power over someone or something, there is little question as to whether a person could ever be in a position to manifest toxicity.

Looking Inward

Toxic teachers might be the best teachers on campus. Furthermore, toxic teachers might even be popular among faculty and colleagues. Yet, underneath it all, there is a particular part of their personality that emerges in their practice and illustrates something serious, resulting in negative effects on others. Some label this expression as *an air of arrogance*. Others find a certain set of traits that border on narcissism. Still others find that there is an undercurrent of negativity that follows the teacher and, in the presence of others, the vibes are plainly felt. A toxic teacher is more than what he or she does as a teacher. Toxicity manifests itself over time and begins to chip away at relationships and the overall school environment.

Truly toxic teachers can often cover their toxicity by expressing different parts of personalities to just the right people. For example, students may not know they are being exposed to toxins when they take sides in a class, or are exposed to viewpoints that are diametrically in opposition to the ways their parents are rearing them at home. They might consider it a novel teaching approach or *cool content*. Newer faculty may not be aware of the veteran teacher's toxic manipulation as he or she steps forward in support of one teacher over another or are mentioned by one considered as toxic.

Parents might not see the evidence of a toxic teacher, and, certainly, administrators sometimes tend to be either too busy or too ignorant of the teacher's toxicity. "Often, these educators are not outright bad. They can be popular with particular groups of students and parents. They can appear effective in the classroom but have no desire to exceed baseline expectations or take on new challenges."² But what exactly brings people to the point of slapping the label of toxic on a colleague?

Before a teacher is labeled as toxic, there must be some key elements considered. Debbie Silver writes about some of these elements, which include "dissimilarities in learning styles, introversion vs. extroversion, and even generational differences."³ What may be considered toxic to a veteran teacher might not be the case to the younger teachers. In fact, being labeled toxic by someone equally can be considered as toxic itself.

Toxic Norms

There are differences in *teaching about* topics and *teaching from within* topics. Good teachers teach about and do so from various perspectives. This approach gains the confidence of fair-minded students and parents, especially those in middle school and above. But schools that promote stories to first graders about alternative lifestyles, without balancing the reality of most families as the norm, can be considered by parents as activism. This is what is meant by the term *teaching from within* topics.

There is motivation to normalize something that is considered by most as outside the norm. The fact that a teacher would even mention the word *norm* today when speaking of mothers and fathers is often enough to evoke anger. One of the better examples of how school culture has become affected by teachers' personal views is the increase of educators now lobbying for full inclusion of every family type in unique fashion.

Teachers are being told by advocacy groups and their districts not to refer to parents as mothers and fathers. Rather, they are being instructed to refer to them as *special persons in their lives*. In the name of inclusion, the references to biological parents and traditional families are diminished, and students from these homes may never hear about the traditional family as nuclear and historical. For example, Elizabeth Mulvahill points out that for schools "it's not really necessary to designate an event for moms only or dads only, etc. What's important is for students to be able to include someone they care about in a special school event."⁴

While this is a current wave in society, there is nothing toxic about celebrating those families who are intact and have risen above the cultural changes and remain in public schools. The fact that so many families are fractured is evidence of toxicity in American culture.

A recent example of this is the group of parents who shared their concerns at a local meeting attended by this author. The parents' comments are relevant as they place teachers squarely in the direct line of fire for the contexts of experiences that are present in their classrooms. One parent commented about her traditional, nuclear family saying, "I feel like every living arrangement and alternative family structure is more important than mine."

Teachers advocating for certain social causes run the risk of being viewed as toxic teachers by those in disagreement. Fair teaching on these topics requires wisdom and balance.

As the reader delves into the issue of toxic teachers, there should be a warning given that teaching toxic topics or stirring up controversial issues in certain classes does not necessarily mean a teacher is toxic. Sometimes, people just do not click with one another.

Sometimes, teachers may be under mandates to teach something for which they are blamed by parents. Other times, teachers go against the grain and step out of their collegial roles and become the rogue instructor. Silver argues that people should not be quick to apply negative labels to teachers. She agrees that such a larger perspective would be helpful and that considerations should lead to understanding teachers before "dismissing someone as a toxic person who just needs to be avoided."[5] For additional information see chapter 5 on *toxic teachings*.

SUI: Students under the Influence

Ask any teenager about *being under the influence*, and the person doing the questioning will probably be met with snickers and laughter. There are issues with teenagers experimenting with substances, including drugs, alcohol, vaping, and sex. When it comes to adults, teachers included, any discussion about intoxication is usually greeted with a universal understanding that it is impermissible for teachers to be at work under the influence or intoxicated. However, this injunction pertains to substances that are tangible, often taken by mouth, smoked, injected, or applied. Some of these may be by a physician's prescription. Those conditions aside, however, toxic teachers usually teach under the influence of their own toxicity, and students usually learn within the context of this same toxicity.

Aside from the insidious drug addiction problems that exist in schools and across the wider swath of American culture, which are addressed in chapter 3, there are subtle psychological and emotional intoxicants that are found in classrooms throughout the nation.

Manipulation of feelings and behaviors are part of what transfers a teacher's toxicity to students. Through instruction, teachers can use the draw strings of race, religion, ethnicity, sex, and gender, and can be either subtly subversive to mainstream classical American culture or interject a continuous stream of progressive ideologies.

One of the reasons private schools and homeschools have surged over the past couple of decades is that parents do not want teachers undermining the values their children receive from home. Students who become persuaded by teachers who are highly persuasive can flip a classroom culture in a very short period of time. Where a spirit of critique and respectful dissent is absent, there is also probably absent objectivity and freedom to speak one's conscience.

Most teachers today are under the influence, meaning that state policy and district mandates govern their actions. Since most teachers are compliant, they go along with the expectations and requirement of the jobs and digest what is expected of them. Along with these requirements and mandates, teachers under the influence can either transmit or withhold political values of bureaucrats and elected officials, thereby extending greater influence to their students.

The teachers who apply a conscientious approach toward shaping the world views of their students are those who exert influence upon the values of these same students. Here is where parents might view such teachers as presenting views toxic to the values of their families. A sure sign that students are under the influence of a teacher's instruction is whether they begin to challenge or refute their parents' values, based on their teacher's instruction. This is why two elements must be considered when addressing toxicity in the classroom and its influence upon students. These two elements are (1) teachers beliefs and (2) the content taught by the teachers.

Toxic conflicts emerge when this content is outside the perspectives of the values taught at home.

An Example of Influence
Recently, the state of California joined other states in changing its history and sex education curriculum to include LGBTQ+ history and lifestyles. The effect of this change in California was a number of parents from the Rocklin School District removing their students from school in protest.[6]

Parents were angry, but little could be done since the political makeup of the school board, the state legislature, and the power of LGBTQ+ lobbies at the state level wield legislative power. The parents who argued against the curriculum were viewed as toxic parents, disliking people of alternate lifestyles, while these same parents viewed the LGBTQ+ community, the legislature, and the school board's actions as toxic.

There was an increase in the outcry of some of the California school district parents who were not allowed to opt their children out of the curricula.[7] California is now one of four politically progressive-led states that require schools to teach LGBTQ+ history or lifestyle practices in sex-education curriculum.[8]

This begs the question as to whether a teacher immediately is branded with the label *toxic* if he or she refused to teach the curriculum on religious grounds or refused not to teach it on the grounds of personal disdain for LGBTQ+ identity.[9] The chances that he or she would be either fired or reassigned have now increased in California and other states.[10] What is mandated by a state is required to be taught. Regardless, some parents viewed this mandate as a means to socially engineer their children to a political point of view.

California public schools are becoming toxic environments, driven by agenda from both political and social policies that are not in line with a vast number of Californians.[11] However, according to the Sacramento LGBTQ+ Community Center spokeswoman, Rachel Henry, "There are several empirical studies that show textbook curriculum that is explicitly inclusive of the LGBTQ+ has dramatically positive effects on school climate for both LGBTQ+ and non-LGBTQ+ students. Students of marginalized groups, such as the LGBTQ+ community, have a right to see themselves reflected in the history that they study."[12] This serves to illustrate an earlier point as to the importance of understanding that it is sometimes difficult to separate toxic teachings from the teachers. Again, for additional discussion on this matter, see chapter 5.

Action Civics

Public school teachers are beginning to realize the importance of training students in what is now being referred to as "action civics." This is intentional and is a by-product of social-emotional learning programs.[13] In the words of Joan Duffell, of the Committee for Children (CFC), "SEL is not only fundamental to education, but it's fundamental to raising citizens who actually participate in democratic life."[14] The only question is what political and social direction will these active students lean? Would civic-minded students be celebrated as successful in their SEL programs if they turned out not to fit the mold socially and politically?

The purpose of action civics is clear. The purpose is to turn "anger into legislative action"[15] on their behalf. Students in elementary schools are being instructed on how to fight for their causes and ways to present their causes to legislators so that they can persuade elected officials to change government. Every topic from AIDS and HIV requirements, sex education, LGBTQ+

inclusion, to immigration, and others are being explored through action civics. The bottom line is that some teachers are now trainers of political and social activists and harnessing students' emotions for civic engagement.[16] This should never be the ultimate purpose of education. Yet, by emphasizing the social and emotional sides of students, what else could one expect but actions that would follow?[17]

One of the upsides of teaching students to advocate for themselves and to change laws on their behalf is the realization of empowerment. Students taking ownership of their citizenship in positive ways benefits the nation in the long run. One of the downsides is, unless the empowerment respects all views, including those with political and social differences, then slanted bias results. Critics fear teachers of social-emotional learning will decide that rhetoric and beliefs of religious dissenters, for example, should not be tolerated and that public schools should take the reins "in case the parents and church don't do it right—perhaps teaching the wrong attitudes and mindsets."[18]

In terms of social and emotional learning, advocates and critics see the injections of social issues and questionable curriculum as both positive and negative.[19] On the other hand, there are objections concerning the rights teachers have in using the emotions of students as motivation. Should teachers get them to act on behalf of causes and issues that are by themselves toxic in nature? On the other hand, what are the obligations of today's public school educators in assisting students toward the development of good citizenship?

Whether it is a philosophy based in activism or a teacher making certain to communicate alternate lifestyles, some teachers may be teaching under the influence of themselves. Care needs to be exercised when teaching outside of what many parents anticipate as good education for their children.

The question to be considered then is: Is it acceptable to educate children with the intention of producing adherents and followers of any of these influences? Toxic teachers may be more inclined to say yes!

Understanding Teacher Toxicity

The meaning of the word *toxic* depends much on the context in which it is applied. For example, something that is toxic includes containing or being poisonous material especially when capable of causing death or serious debilitation to exhibiting symptoms of infection or that which is extremely harsh, malicious, or harmful. There are others, including synonyms, such as the adjectival terms envenomed, poisoned, venomous, and so on.[20]

In more general terms, hyperbole and exaggeration also qualify as contexts for defining the term. Toxicity can be applied to the actions of people and their manipulation or the creation of an environment that could cause emotional or psychological upset. Within this context, what signs would indicate whether or not a teacher is toxic?

The Trickiness of Teacher Toxicity

The following indicators are not meant to serve as a checklist. In some ways, indications of toxicity are left to the subjective experiences of people. Therefore, what is toxic to one, may not be toxic to another. Consider the brash East Coast persona stereotype and the laid-back Southerner and how they might view each other. Toxicity is sometimes difficult to nail down in a bullet point.

The chances are that the brash type A–driven personality, which accompanies straightforward brutish expressions of feelings on issues, might be toxic to a person more reserved. However, to another East Coast person, there might be no offense taken whatsoever by the actions of the more relaxed stereotype of the Southerner.

For example, transplanted teachers from the Northeastern United States can attest to a misconception—which often leads to misunderstanding—of personality types. Those from the aggressive *tri-state* region that includes New York, New Jersey, and Connecticut come saddled with a stereotypical reputation. But this region is not alone.

According to a 2013 *Journal of Personality and Social Psychology*, there are three types of people in the United States,[21] which are based on the regions where they live. First is *the friendly and conventional region*. Second is *the relaxed and creative region*. Third is *the temperamental and uninhibited region*.

Within each of these types of people, there are many teachers. Within each teacher pool, there are no doubts some teachers who are considered toxic. One can only wonder how toxic inhabitants of the temperamental and uninhibited region come across to inhabitants of the other two regions.

There must be considerations as to whether a teacher is toxic and to whom this toxicity is directed. A general question might be asked whether the teacher is affecting students, fellow teachers, the spirit of the campus, parental relationships, or any combination of these.

Something else to consider is that disagreeable people may not be toxic at all. Disagreements occur when people work together; working through disagreements is a hallmark of a good workplace environment. Working out solutions to problems is a plus and actually avoids the development of problems down the road.

Likewise, a loud, provocative teacher—one who demonstrates passion for learning in a classroom—is not necessarily toxic in his or her role as a teacher. Yet in a faculty meeting or a meeting with parents, this same teacher might well exhibit a confrontational nature deemed toxic, which is kept under wraps in the classroom. In America today, teachers have to guard against negative labels placed on them by people whose experiences with them are few.

Difficulty in Defining the Toxic Teacher

For the reasons just stated, it is incumbent on professionals not to place colleagues into boxes for one thing or another in their styles, behaviors, and personalities. Tight definitions must apply to toxicity so as to avoid the contemporary urban and unpolished definition of toxicity. However, a more general, practical definition is appropriate at this juncture.

In general, toxic people are those who are "rude and can't be nice. They are not true to people around them. They need an attitude check. Their personalities are so unappealing it makes the people around them suffer and turn rude as well."[22] Therefore, is a teacher toxic because of the recipient's feelings around that person, or are there objective measures to assist in drawing such a conclusion? Does a toxic teacher have to be toxic to all colleagues and administrators, an entire school and object environment, and all students and parents to be truly toxic? The answer is that, if this were the case, it would certainly make pinning down toxicity much easier. This is evidence that pinning down a toxic teacher with a strict definition or absolute traits is tricky and ill-advised.

Administrators and Toxic Teachers

The overall expectations and professional demands placed on teachers is highly stressful, and there are days when negativity and pessimism abound on some campuses. Therefore,

> in order to stay positive in this challenging profession, it is imperative that we as educators surround ourselves with others who believe we can make a difference and that what we do matters. We can't always choose the people with whom we work, but we can learn to identify the talking snakes and cut them a wide path.[23]

Toxic teachers are challenges to school administrators. They are challenges for several reasons. The first challenge to an administrator is to identify those faculty members who have toxic tendencies and determine why. Once these teachers are identified, administrators can begin to develop strategies for which to deal with them. Countering negativity and pessimism, as well as toxicity, means remaining above the fray while countering the issue of toxicity. It is best to remember that toxic teachers may not be toxic as people. There may be causes of the toxicity that may need to be addressed positively.

To this end, Amelia Harper shares four commonsense, basic strategies for administrators dealing with toxic teachers. *First*, administrators should build "relationships and rapport with all staff members."[24] *Second*, administrators must be swift and decisive in identifying and "tackling problems early rather than ignoring them."[25] *Third*, when a teacher needs to be approached about something toxic, the meeting between the administrator and the teacher(s) involved should occur in "a private setting."[26] *Fourth*, administrators should be taking regular inventory of themselves to see whether "their own moods, attitudes, and behaviors"[27] may be contributing to the problems associated with toxicity on their school campuses.

What about Triggers?
Not everything who triggers a reaction from a person should be branded as toxic. Today's students are quick to use labels, and social media assists their snap judgments. There are warm-hearted people who are hurt by the least of things. These folks are referred to as *sponges of empathy* and are often hypersensitive. Sometimes, it does not take much to trigger such a person. Consider that more and more teachers are entering the workforce with this hypersensitivity. More often than not, these folks are criticized for their perspective on toxicity, which amounts to *anything that makes me feel like I am offended, uncomfortable, or emotional because of disagreement.*

One of the more interesting traits that teachers point out about toxic colleagues is that they can come across as supportive while elsewhere undercutting people and programs behind the scenes. *The bottom line is there is no one profile of a toxic teacher and no one trigger that demonstrates this toxicity.* There are only senses about words and gestures and actions observed by the recipients that imply toxicity to a person or group.

The term *toxic* is overused as much as the word *racist* so that both words have lost so much meaning by their inapplicable and rampant usage. One person's toxicity is another person's brashness, as any US regional transplant may experience.

Humans are not static, and each day brings with it new challenges to the elements faced in schools. Teachers should look within themselves to see whether there is anything toxic in their personality or practice. Then and only then should teachers begin to identify the traits of toxicity in others.

Are You a Toxic Teacher?

The construction of a set of identifiers for toxic teachers requires self-reflection. This self-reflection takes into account past experiences of (1) resistance to change because of several previously failed changes, (2) being physically and emotionally burned out, (3) disagreeability or oppositional nature, and (4) personality conflicts with colleagues or administrators.[28] Some toxic teachers develop over time, while others already seem to be in such a state when they arrive on the job.

Toxic teachers can "wield negative power in schools, corrupting the culture and causing problems for principals, parents, and students."[29] A toxic teacher must learn to analyze his or her behaviors and come to understand some of the triggers for them. Toxic teachers can also feel empowered to speak their minds. In the process, the toxic teacher may exhibit signs of concern. Taken as a group, the teacher may (1) be consistently confrontational, (2) appear sometimes unapproachable, (3) blame others for shortcomings, (4) talk one way about faculty and another way to parents, (5) enable wedges to sever collegial relationships, (6) foster negativity, (7) compete in a noncompetitive environment, (8) have narcissistic tendencies, (9) practice sarcasm, and (10) be given to general pessimism.

Disillusionment

Some toxic teachers suffer from disillusionment about schooling and the system, and they could lack excitement about working with students every day—even going to work may have lost its appeal. Likewise, there may be a loss of the teacher's sense of calling or purpose. This type of teacher is buried in the chores of schooling and focuses on making it through the day. The longer the career, the more often the teacher is found to be counting down the years until retirement.

A once promising career might now be compromised. Life's calling feels more like a job. The toxic teacher will sometimes share disillusionment about work with students and might even use his or her platform as a catharsis. Venting, griping, and sarcasm begin to define the toxic teacher, and these expressions infect the classroom environment. The teacher ultimately feels stuck in the job, and this begins to fester.

Toxic teachers may suffer from a loss of passion and no longer give of themselves to their students as they once did. Such a teacher may also be experiencing burnout, feel overused, and be unable to find balance between his or her professional and personal lives. This is where the overwhelming expectations of education and the responsibilities become more than they can handle.

In the words of Jamy Brice-Hyde, a New York teacher, "Nobody realizes how horrific working conditions are for teachers throughout the country."[30] Three teachers who were a part of a network to which Brice-Hyde belongs committed suicide, just a few weeks apart, bringing to light just how stressful the job of education can be.[31]

Some toxic teachers can be found working under great stress physically and emotionally. This is evidenced by surveys taken by teacher advocacy groups and unions. The annual surveys of teachers from the National Education Association (NEA) and the American Federation of Teachers demonstrate the seriousness of the problem.

The social media group Badass Teachers Association (BAT), a grassroots teachers' activist group of over two hundred thousand members, partnered with the AFT to survey the mood and experiences of teachers' working conditions across the nation. The name of the document produced was titled "2017 Educator Quality of Work Life Survey."[32] The survey results demonstrated that "sixty-one percent of educators find work 'always' or 'often' stressful. Twenty-seven percent of educators said they've been threatened, bullied, or harassed. Eighty-six percent of educators feel disrespected by U.S. Secretary of Education Betsy DeVos. Teachers are stressed out and turnover is high."[33]

Cynicism
Toxic teachers may begin to develop a cynical side and to engage the challenges of the workplace over the education of the students. As a result, the lens of toxicity begins to focus on the worst in people and circumstances. This means that the cynical teacher sees the worst in students and is driven by a sense of pessimism and sarcasm.

Every teacher who has been around awhile has horror stories about one class or another. Those type of classes bring classroom toxicity to new heights. In classes such as these, when things go awry, the toxic's cynicism enables the development or continuation of an environment that is fueled by an *attitude of battletude*.

This attitude can lead to the development of something quite damaging over time. For example, when students tend to fall short in what is academically or behaviorally expected of them, the students are made to feel inadequate. Toxic teachers make negative comments to colleagues that the students just might not be smart enough, do not try hard enough, or fail because their families come from a culture where education is simply not that important. Some toxic teachers do not take the blame for the shortcomings of the students. Therefore, such a teacher is described as one who harms or dismisses children by words, actions, reactions, emotions, body language, targeted physical discipline, or inappropriate relationships.[34]

Thus, the toxic teacher becomes disengaged in the personal responsibility of learning in such a toxic environment, which becomes the crowning achievement of cynicism. This leads to the next sign for which to be aware.

Ruler of Information
The toxic teacher takes pride in being first with the on-campus gossip. As with most toxic teachers, there is a certain power that is attractive to the person with information that piques the interest of others when it is disseminated. The toxic gossiper feels empowered by the sense of ownership over a private pipeline of information. More often than not, the focus of gossip by a toxic teacher is almost always of the salacious or negative side-taking variety.

Sometimes, toxic teachers announce good news, which is equally meant to grab attention. Gossip can be both a contagion and an incendiary at the same time. When asked where most of the gossip on school campuses takes place, there are usually three responses: (1) the teachers' lounge; (2) the parking lot with parents; and (3) the Internet, specifically social media, where gossip tends to run unchecked.

Toxic gossip has been called many things over the years, and it continues to occur wherever teachers congregate. Teachers spend countless early mornings and late afternoons making photocopies for their classes. Even in the age of classroom technology of iPads or Chromebooks, teachers still prefer hard copies for some subjects. As a means to attract those of like mind, the toxic teacher may take the lead in complaining about students. Lauren Vargas puts it this way: "As a teacher, I spent many mornings in line to make copies for my lessons that day. Coffee in hand, I competed with my fellow colleagues in the Misery Olympics of Teaching: We'd banter back and forth about whose teaching life was more miserable."[35]

This type of toxic conversation is upscaled once the teacher becomes an administrator at a school and there is a natural pulling away of the administrator from the teaching ranks. Faculty who are fearful for having gossiped with a one-time colleague now walk on egg shells, fearful of possible retribution from the new administrator.[36]

Certainly, the stress is extremely high in public schools today, and some of these types of conversations are meant as humorous. Other conversations occur in efforts to blow off steam. However, toxicity can be couched in humor or sewn into the fabric of a teacher's expectations placed on them by others.

Who Is More Toxic?

Are male or female teachers more toxic? The fact is that there are more women in the teaching profession, so numbers would indicate women, by that figure. However, it would not be politically correct to label one or the other as more gossipy since the word is "not gender specific."[37] The safest answer to this query is that humans are toxic, but it is just that they do not think they are.[38]

In reference to gossip, a recent study published in the *Social Psychological and Personality Science* (SPPS) journal concluded:

> Frequent gossipers tended to be more extraverted. Women engaged in more neutral gossip than men, and younger people tended to negatively gossip more than older people. Gossip tended to be neutral, rather than positive or negative, and about social information. These naturalistic observation findings dispel some stereotypes about this prevalent yet misunderstood behavior.[39]

When it comes to gossip, both women and men of all ages can be equal opportunity offenders and, therefore, open to constructing or adding to toxic school environments. So the question now is asked whether toxic teachers are more inclined toward gossip, or are gossipers more inclined toward being toxic? The answer is probably yes to both, on some level. However, the SPPS study also revealed that "although laypeople often view gossipers as immoral, uneducated, typically female, and of lower social class, no systematic observation has empirically revealed the characteristics of those who gossip more than others nor examined the characteristics of gossip across everyday contexts."[40]

Disagreement and Dissent

The toxic teacher is known to practice disagreement and dissent. For example, a book written to mock Vice President Mike Pence's position against same-sex marriage was read by a Sanford, Florida, public school teacher to his first-grade class.[41] Parents felt "this was not appropriate for the young students"[42] and that it had not "been run by the parents first."[43] Toxic teachers take it upon themselves to demonstrate disagreement and dissent, sometimes at the expense of their students' emotions.

One should expect the same outcry if books ridiculing same-sex marriage, abortion, or transgenderism were read to public school students without parents' knowledge and without the possibility for parents to opt their children out. Again, flip around the approach and consider the horror over books being read to students belittling former Vice President Joseph Biden.

Toxic teachers can also leave students frustrated and discontent. Sometimes, students' frustrations are the results of a teacher's verbal expressions and sardonic statements. This became an issue in public schools with the election of President Obama and continues in schools with the Trump administration.[44] There is natural toxicity in politics that brings out the worst in many people.

The Entrenched

Activist teachers for one thing or another comprise one side of toxicity. The other side of toxicity can be just as problematic. Sometimes, toxic teachers are opposed to change and feel under no moral obligation to change their ways, unless it is the law. Such teachers see no need for changing what they know is *right and works*, regardless of the law.

Toxic teachers feel successful with what is done and how it is accomplished. In fact, this is the way they have always done it, and there is no need to change the method—and this includes extra work from home.[45] The younger generation of teachers seeking to make bold moves and radical changes in teaching and classroom management can easily view this entrenchment as toxic. So toxic teachers are not just proactive or reactive to change. Toxicity can also be *non-active*.

Effects of Teacher Toxicity on Students

Teachers are a savvy bunch and usually know what takes place within their schools and between teachers and administrators. However, there are times when teachers are unaware of their personal effects on their schools, colleagues, students, and parents. For example, how many teachers have ever wondered why one or two of their colleagues always seem to elicit eye rolls at faculty meetings? Ever question why others sit quietly and never question a particular colleague or administrator over a suggestion or idea? If any of the answers to these questions is connected to *fear*, then there is the basis for a toxic environment.

Toxic teachers have the ability to produce negative stress on the brains of their students. "More than half of all students in U.S. public schools come from low-income families. Poverty is associated with chronic stress, which can have a toxic effect on the brain."[46] A teacher who does not understand this runs the risk of adding stressors to already toxic brains.

That being said. Not all stress is bad.

> Stress can help us stay alert and adapt to changes around us. Tolerable stressors give us energy and strength—through increased metabolism and heightened

bodily response—to get a job done. With toxic stress, however, there is no relief. The stress is ongoing and unremitting. The "fight-or-flight" hormone levels remain elevated for extended periods of time, which negatively affects the body and the brain.[47]

Human brains rely on experiences, repetition, and emotional and cognitive recognition. The human brain

> is an experience-dependent organ; it gets better at what it does most. With chronic toxic stress, the brain is focused on and therefore over-exercising its stress responses (fight or flight). When that happens, the brain is preparing us to act quickly and decisively, with no time for thinking about the problem. That's why the student who has experienced toxic stress reacts more impulsively to potential stressors, including those that may not bother someone else at all, such as an accidental bump on the shoulder or a comment from a teacher. The student also remains agitated for a much longer time. This can translate to highly impulsive behavior, increased aggression, or what may appear to be a lack of self-control and poor listening skills. The student is on high alert at all times, which can be problematic in a classroom. In essence, the "thinking" brain is blocked, so it is not exercising skills needed to do well in areas like math, reading, or problem solving.[48]

Teachers must continually be aware of the triggers of stress to the brains of their students. They must understand the nature of trauma in the lives of the developing brains of their students. All things considered, is this not another argument for children and teenagers not to make life-altering decisions based on trauma, turmoil, or confusion in their lives—even if encouraged to do so by a teacher?

Dealing with Toxic Teachers

Over time, a toxic environment can be quite infectious and tend to involve other teachers into its web of negativity. Debbie Silver calls toxic teachers *talking snakes*; she recommends several ways to deal with them—especially those who become toxic over time.[49] Teachers seeking to avoid becoming affected by toxic colleagues would do well to remember the following:

- Be polite, but share minimal information about yourself.
- In social situations, do not be willing to join a group they are already in or they frequently attend.
- If the negative person tries to bait you into an argument, take the high ground . . . agree to disagree and walk away.

- Do not gossip.
- Do not force colleagues to take sides.
- Work cordially, knowing there will be times when you cannot avoid the person.
- Focus on students and personal goals, and do not waste time on worrying what the negative people might be saying about you or doing behind your back.

Silver's advice is especially appropriate for new and beginning teachers.

Moving Away from Being a Toxic Teacher

Is it true that once toxic, always toxic? People can change if they want to, or, if they are unaware of their toxicity, a form of intervention as professional development might be able to assist in pointing out areas of toxicity. Teachers are resilient and often perform self-reflection. However, in pointing out areas that need attention, such as personality improvements, team playing, or a form of narcissism deleterious to unity on campus—or even the incendiary comments that strike either fear or cause undue anxiety on the parts of teachers or students—an insecure toxic teacher might then view any such attempt as offensive and toxic in its own right. As a result, very little would then have been accomplished.

Assuming that a toxic teacher is open to change and is willing to work on some areas of his or her life and apply improvements, what exactly would an intervention need to include? A school with a supportive and balanced administrator is a plus. The ability of an administrator to balance the contention and see the core of an issue while respecting people over the issues is critical. The intervention is already set up to fail if the administrators and some teachers are the causes of toxicity. There is no doubt that toxic teachers present some of the more difficult challenges for school administrators.[50] Predictably, some toxic parents are lined up right behind these teachers.

Changing School Culture from the Top

A toxic administrator should be considered in the same light as a toxic teacher. But dealing with administrators is quite different from dealing with teachers. For example, teachers just can't avoid a toxic administrator since the role of the administrator is different from the roles of the teachers. A trait of a toxic administrator is one who manipulates people from all angles while placating, but not solving, the issues that arise.

Ultimately, a toxic administrator will affect overall school culture negatively. For example, consider the principal of an elementary school in an urban area. When called out by two of his faculty for creating a toxic work environment, spurred on by inappropriate relationships with some of his female faculty—and then accused of favoritism for his *pet teachers*—the principal resorted to toxic tactics in retaliation.

The principal refused to acknowledge the existence of his accusers on campus and never set foot into their classrooms for the remainder of the year. The school district offered no disciplinary action, and the toxicity on that elementary campus continued to fester. Eventually, parents and students were taking sides, and social media lit up with additional toxicity.

Toxic administrators are difficult to remove. But teachers cannot be afraid to stand up for their students and parents as well as for their careers. No one should have to work in a toxic environment that is repeatedly harming adults and children. Teachers should remember one thing, "A school's culture is never too late to fix; but it does take a decision to do something about it."[51]

Notes

1. James Madison. "The Federalist No. 10: The utility of the union as a safeguard against domestic faction and insurrection." *Daily Advertiser*. November 22, 1787. Retrieved from https://www.constitution.org/fed/federa10.htm.

2. Staff. "The six signs of a toxic teacher." *The Source*. April 2018. Vol. 15:4. Retrieved from https://isminc.com/blog/academic-leadership/vol-15/no-4/the-six-signs-of-a-toxic-teacher.

3. Debbie Silver. "Dealing with toxic teachers." *Corwin Connect*. September 25, 2014. Retrieved from https://corwin-connect.com/2014/09/dealing-toxic-teachers/.

4. Elizabeth Mulvahill. "Enough with donuts with dads and muffins with moms—Let's make all school events inclusive." *We Are Teachers*. May 31, 2019. Retrieved from https://schoolleadersnow.weareteachers.com/inclusive-school-events/.

5. Debbie Silver. "Dealing with toxic teachers."

6. Neal Broverman. "Hundreds of parents pull kids from school to protest LGBTQ+ curriculum." May 8, 2019. *The Advocate*. Retrieved from https://www.advocate.com/news/2019/5/08/hundreds-parents-pull-kids-school-protest-lgbtq-curriculum.

7. Mary Margaret Olohan. "California school district will not allow parents to opt children out of LGBTQ content, emails show." *Daily Caller*. August 13, 2019. Retrieved from https://dailycaller.com/2019/08/13/california-school-lgbtq-content/. Cf. Hannan Adely. "Can parents opt out of New Jersey's LGBTQ curriculum law?" *North Jersey Record*. June 26, 2019. Retrieved from https://www.northjersey.com/story/news/education/2019/06/26/teaching-lgbtq-in-schools-can-nj-parents-opt-out/1549151001/.

8. Sarah Schwartz. "Four states now require schools to teach LGBT history." *Education Week*. August 12, 2019. Retrieved from http://blogs.edweek.org/teachers/teaching_now/2019/08/four_states_now_require_schools_to_teach_lgbt_history.html.

9. Michelle L. Page. "From awareness to action: Teacher attitude and implementation of LGBT-inclusive curriculum in the English–Language Arts classroom." *Sage Open Journal*. October–December 2017, pp. 1–15. Retrieved from https://journals.sagepub.com/doi/pdf/10.1177/2158244017739949.

10. Ibid.

11. Ricardo Cano. "California schools haven't fully embraced laws protecting LGBTQ kids, study shows." *Cal Matters*. May 13, 2019. Retrieved from https://calmatters.org/education/2019/05/california-transgender-schools-lgbtq-laws-education-civil-rights/.

12. Neal Broverman. "Hundreds of parents pull kids from school to protest LGBTQ curriculum."

13. Catherine Gewertz. "Action civics enlists students in hands-on democracy." *Education Week*. March 20, 2019. Retrieved from https://www.edweek.org/ew/articles/2019/03/20/action-civics-enlists-students-in-hands-on-democracy.html.

14. Victoria Clayton. "The psychological approach to educating kids." *Atlantic*. March 30, 2017. Retrieved from https://www.theatlantic.com/education/archive/2017/03/the-social-emotional-learning-effect/521220/.

15. Catherine Gewertz. "Action civics enlists students in hands-on democracy."

16. Brenda Iasevoli. "Harnessing student emotions in service of a cause." *Education Week*. June 7, 2017. Retrieved from https://www.edweek.org/tm/articles/2017/06/07/harnessing-student-emotions-in-service-of-a.html?qs=social+emotional+learning+in+service+of+a+cause.

17. Karen R. Effrem. "How 'social emotional learning' is turning children into leftist activists." *The National Pulse*. June 23, 2017. Retrieved from https://thenationalpulse.com/commentary/social-emotional-learning-turning-children-leftist-activists/.

18. Victoria Clayton. "The psychological approach to educating kids." *Atlantic*. March 30, 2017. Retrieved from https://www.theatlantic.com/education/archive/2017/03/the-social-emotional-learning-effect/521220/.

19. Ibid.

20. "Toxic." https://www.merriam-webster.com/dictionary/toxic.

21. Peter J. Rentfrow, Samuel D. Gosling, Markus Jokela, et al. "Divided we stand: Three psychological regions of the United States and their political, economic, social, and health correlates." *Journal of Personality and Social Psychology*. 2013. Vol. 105, No. 6, pp. 996–2012. Retrieved from https://www.apa.org/pubs/journals/releases/psp-a0034434.pdf. Cf. Marina Koren. "The three kinds of people who live in the United States." *Atlantic*. October 23, 2013. Retrieved from https://www.theatlantic.com/national/archive/2013/10/the-three-kinds-of-people-who-live-in-the-united-states/280799/.

22. "Toxic." https://www.urbandictionary.com/define.php?term=Toxic.

23. Debbie Silver. "Dealing with toxic teachers."

24. Amelia Harper. "Toxic teachers present disciplinary challenges to administrators." *Education Dive*. October 22, 2018. Retrieved from https://www.educationdive.com/news/toxic-teachers-present-disciplinary-challenges-to-administrators/540102/.

25. Ibid.

26. Ibid.

27. Ibid.

28. Ibid.

29. Ibid.

30. Stacy Tornio. "We need to do more for teachers who are exhausted, stressed, and burned out." *We Are Teachers*. October 9, 2018. Retrieved from https://www.weareteachers.com/teacher-mental-health/.

31. Ibid.

32. Ibid.

33. Ibid.

34. Carol Bainbridge. "What is a toxic teacher?" *Gifts for Learning*. May 6, 2015. Retrieved from http://giftsforlearning.com/wp/what-is-a-toxic-teacher/.

35. Lauren Vargas. "Complaining about students is toxic. Here are 4 ways to stop." *Education Week*. June 11, 2019. Retrieved from https://www.edweek.org/tm/articles/2019/06/12/complaining-about-students-is-toxic-here-are.html.

36. Jacqueline Burnett-Brown. "Toxic school environments make teachers sick." *Mediate*. May 2017. Retrieved from https://www.mediate.com/articles/BrownJbl20170522.cfm.

37. Staff. "Women vs. men: Who gossips more?" *Everyday Health*. November 15, 2017. Retrieved from https://www.everydayhealth.com/healthy-living/women-vs-men-who-gossips-more/.

38. Chris Matyszczyk. "Men gossip just as much as women, says just published study (and boy, do we spend a lot of time gossiping)." *Inc*. May 17, 2019. Retrieved from https://www.inc.com/chris-matyszczyk/men-gossip-more-negatively-than-women-says-new-study.html.

39. Megan L. Robbins and Alexander Karan. "Who gossips and how in everyday life?" *Social Psychological and Personality Science*. May 2, 2019. Retrieved from https://journals.sagepub.com/doi/abs/10.1177/1948550619837000?journalCode=sppa.

40. Ibid.

41. Kerry Justich. "Parents outraged at first-grade teacher's decisions to read book about gay bunnies to students." *Microsoft News*. February 13, 2019. Retrieved from https://www.msn.com/en-us/news/us/parents-outraged-at-first-grade-teachers-decision-to-read-book-about-gay-bunnies-to-students/ar-BBRkM3j.

42. Ibid.

43. Ibid.

44. Jonathan Zimmerman. "'By the people' critiqued: A textbook case of toxic politics." *The San Francisco Chronicle*. April 28, 2018. Retrieved from https://

www.sfchronicle.com/opinion/article/By-the-People-critiqued-a-textbook-case-of-12868000.php.

45. Staff. "The six signs of a toxic teacher." *The Source*. April 2018. Vol. 15:4. Retrieved from https://isminc.com/blog/academic-leadership/vol-15/no-4/the-six-signs-of-a-toxic-teacher.

46. Martha S. Burns. "Three ways to counter the effects of stress on the brain." *Association of Supervision and Curriculum Development*. January 25, 2018. Retrieved from http://www.ascd.org/ascd-express/vol13/1310-burns.aspx.

47. Ibid.

48. Ibid.

49. Debbie Silver. "Dealing with toxic teachers." Cf. Chad Boender. "5 ways to deal with negative teachers." No Date. *Hey Teach!* Retrieved from https://www.wgu.edu/heyteach/article/5-ways-deal-negative-teachers1712.html.

50. Amelia Harper. "Toxic teachers present disciplinary challenges to administrators."

51. Pernille Ripp. "When a school becomes toxic—What can we do to change school culture?" *Author Blog*. February 14, 2016. Retrieved from https://pernillesripp.com/2016/02/14/when-a-school-becomes-toxic-what-can-we-do-to-change-school-cultureul/.

CHAPTER FIVE

Toxic Teachings

> Suppose the government decides a child will be a more acceptable student, citizen, and worker bee if he learns to acquiesce to the "consensus" of the group, regardless of his own moral standards, or if she learns to accept that all commands of the government must be obeyed. The student may fulfill the standard by developing the correct attitudes, but under whose authority does the government presume to instill attitudes that may conflict with parents' desires?
>
> —Jane Robbins[1]

The recent literature on toxicity in public schools deals more with personalities and student bullying than it does with the actual material presented from the curriculum or at the lesson selectivity level of the classroom teacher. However, along with this literature, teacher anecdotes, new state curricula, and over forty years of personal experience in education, the conclusion is that classroom instruction is becoming toxic in its own way.

Toxic Indicators

What follows is a list of ten characteristics and indicators that are most often predominant within toxic teachings. They are

1. fragmentation and marginalization of the unity of the classroom by group status of race, ethnicity, education, or economics;
2. social divisiveness through sarcasm, name-calling, and labeling;

3. practicing slanted-issue teacher advocacy and select curriculum viewpoint bias;
4. political partisanship;
5. foundation of emotional expressions as determinants of truth while negating competing emotions as untrue;
6. inciting of explicit side taking and tolerating of group shaming;
7. affirming disunity of society in general and blaming groups as scapegoats;
8. driving wedges between people's beliefs and questioning their practices at the expense of their self-esteem and classroom unity;
9. shaming of people and positions that do not fit an emerging agenda or preconceived set of beliefs and practices; and
10. creating a narrative that there are good guys and bad guys on issues and using select media platforms to advance group messaging.

Would a teacher knowingly teach toxic material if he or she were not already motivated toward such an approach? Another question is equally as important. Is it likely that toxic teachings can occur without a teacher's knowledge or be resident in his or her personality or teaching style? Answering yes to both questions brings attention to curricular content.

Teacher Gets Personal
Consider the teacher who made an erroneous choice at the beginning of the 2018–2019 academic school year and used a lesson that was not approved by the school or district to open the subject of transgenderism. Imagine also that students were given the task to explore each other's ideas about sex, gender, and relationships as an introductory activity to the school year.

Well, this does not have to be imagined. The principal of the school at which this occurred "spotted the worksheet during a routine class visit [and] immediately ordered [the teacher] to stop distributing it."[2] The "get to know each other lesson"[3] was shut down after the very first period of the day because of immediate complaints to parents by students, obviously made into more of a problem as students used their cell phones in class.[4]

Although the activity was not an assignment and the students were not obligated to fill out the worksheet, the teacher did not first get permission from the principal to use the material in his classes. The teacher claimed that one of his students was a transgender middle schooler and thought that the activity would benefit students to understand gender identity and sexual attraction more clearly. How does a teacher really know a 12- to 14-year-old is transgender? In the words of one irate parent, "I don't care what you identify as. . . . NO ONE has the right to ask my child these questions."[5]

Assuming the teacher's transgender identity lesson was not creating a hostile environment for students and their families and that the teacher was truly not trying to engineer students toward accepting transgenderism, then this is an example of a toxic lesson that came from a non-toxic teacher. These assumptions would be difficult to decipher since it was the very first day of school for the year. Regardless of the teacher's motivation, parents questioned whether it is a school's role to present and then actively promote such a toxic social cause in the name of education.

Such content and actions on the part of this teacher fulfill several of the indicators listed at the beginning of this chapter and qualify as toxic. Teachings that fragment, marginalize, and undermine unity of the community's values, whether at home or at school, can be deemed toxic.

Fragmentation and Marginalization

Throughout the course of American history there have been many issues that have come between citizens. Some of these included racial and ethnic tensions, economic and financial disparities, and opportunities and level playing fields for minorities and women. McCarthyism, wars, and so many other issues can also be named. In some ways, the issues of the past are still with the nation today. But today's issues come with a type of subterfuge.

Psychologists and other professionals inform teachers that each of them has implicit biases on some levels. In other ways, there is a refashioning of issues of the past, and this new packaging is beneath the surface of the teacher's conscious awareness. Teachers are told that problems found in history are kept alive merely by their being of a certain demographic. A simple rephrasing amounts to *since you exist, you have these traits by default*. As the colloquialism goes, keeping the past alive in the present helps to point out places where the past *is* the present.[6]

White Fragility

Robin DiAngelo, the author of *White Fragility*,[7] helps lead workplace seminars on race. Her approach is

> often met with silence, defensiveness, argumentation, certitude, and other forms of pushback. To explain this phenomenon, she coined the phrase "white fragility.". . . DiAngelo sees white people as singularly responsible [since] only whites have the collective social and institutional power and privilege over people of color . . . [and] she is unimpressed by white participants who swear they "treat everyone the same," since that's not possible.[8]

Teaching about racism today is less about actions and more about a "widely encompassing term of description."⁹ People can disagree on whether actions are racially motivated or not. But, if a person is not a person of color, he or she carries the past as excess baggage and has racism embedded in his or her cultural DNA. Obviously, not everyone sees racism the same way in terms of definitions, actions, and effects. But DiAngelo does bring the conversation front and center.

Ibram Kendi, in *How to Be an Antiracist*, views DiAngelo's perspective from a slightly different angle. He writes

> some unusual but necessary observations, including that characterizing all white people as racist hurts black people. "Racist power thrives on anti-white racist ideas—more hatred only makes their power greater. . . . going after white people instead of racist power prolongs the policies harming black life. In the end, anti-white racist ideas, in taking some or all of the focus off racist power, become anti-black. In the end, hating white people becomes hating black people."¹⁰

Kendi also makes an excellent point in terms of using broad strokes to indict people.

Each era in American history is unique. Twenty-first-century America is no exception. In fact, along with this uniqueness of events, there is always a generation or two who have no recollections of the past, aside from what they are able to read in books or digest on social media. This is where an impressionable generation can be affected by theories and presuppositions that emerge from within progressive culture.

What is common across all of history in terms of teaching is that the fresher the issues, the more impacting the content of the issues can be on the developing minds and hearts of today's students. This is how views can be shaped and minds molded.

What is also common is that far too many students are beginning to feel marginalized in our public schools. When marginal views are either accepted or rejected, a certain number of students feel left out. In a sense, more and more students are *being* marginalized if they fall outside the current progressive social trends, and others *feel* marginalized while inside others.¹¹ It is the teacher's job to level the field of learning.

Teaching Toxic Social Issues

In terms of social issues, most of the nation is dichotomous. Politically, the nation is also somewhat evenly split. Only a small percentage of voters remains in the middle on issues and candidates. Voter registrations and election results demonstrate this.

Teachers who intentionally influence children toward either an emerging social issue or toward a political party become part of what others perceive as toxic. Someone will always be offended by one thing or another. However, generally speaking, teachers should take note of the topics that may result in high levels of toxicity and try to avoid these topics. The higher the levels of toxicity, the more extreme the emotional reactions.

In order to assist teachers, table 5.1 is provided. The table categorizes toxic issues in American schools across levels of toxicity and levels of emotion.

Squarely in the middle of these issues are over fifty million American students. American public schools have become so much more than places

Table 5.1. Toxic Issues in American Schools

Emotionally Extreme	Emotional	Agitation
Highly Toxic Issues	Moderately Toxic Issues	Slightly Toxic Issues
Issues Resulting in Highly Toxic Environments:	Issues Resulting in Moderately Toxic Environments:	Issues Resulting in Slightly Toxic Environments:
Bullying	Academic Curriculum	Academics
Drug and Alcohol Abuse	Affirmative Action	Curriculum
First Amendment Rights	Athletics	Free/Reduced Lunch
Gossiping and Backbiting	Charter Schools	Internet Access
Government and Politics	Classroom Management	Allergies and Food
Identity Movement	Climate Change	Recess
Immigration; Border Control	Environmentalism	Standardized Tests
Intergenerational Trauma	National Infrastructure	Veganism
LGBTQ+	Nepotism	
Poverty	Oppositional Defiance	
Pro-Abortion; Pro-Life	Parent Complaints	
Race, Racism, and Ethnicity	Private vs. Public School	
Same-Sex Marriage	Recreational Drugs	
Second Amendment Rights	Restorative Justice	
Sex Education	Smartphones	
Sexual Orientation	Taxes	
Social Justice	Teacher Shortages	
Socialism and Communism	Unemployment	
Supremacy and Nationalism		
Unconscious Bias		
Voting Rights		
White Privilege		

to send children for an academic education. Almost all public schools have now become completely sold out to the social agency model of educating the whole child. How did this happened? Parts of the child are by necessity of greater attention than others, and some receive no attention.

Public schooling in so many communities, especially inner-city communities, are now welfare institutions with comprehensive services that extend beyond the original purposes meant for education. On its face, the notion that caring for a child's every need, in every way possible, sounds like the most responsible thing to do. But nothing could be further from the truth—especially in caring for the needs of boys in America.

Toxic Masculinity
Colleen Clemens lays out the meaning of the term *toxic masculinity* when she writes,

> Toxic masculinity is tricky. It's a phrase that—misunderstood—can seem wildly insulting, even bigoted. . . . Because the term requires careful contextualization and provokes such strong reactions, our impulse may be to avoid discussing it with our classes. As educators, however, it is our responsibility not to hide from difficult topics or concepts, but to clarify them.[12]

Furthermore, Clemens writes about the controversial topic of brain differences among genders and concludes that *gender identity is a deeply held feeling*.

> Researchers have shown that there is very little difference between the brains of men and women. While gender identity is a deeply held feeling of being male, female, or another gender, people of different genders often act differently, not because of biological characteristics but because of rigid social norms created around femininity and masculinity.[13]

The term *toxic masculinity* is a phrase that "is derived from studies that focus on violent behavior perpetrated by men, and—this is key—is designed to describe not masculinity itself, but a form of gendered behavior that results when expectations of 'what it means to be a man' go wrong."[14]

The *Good Men Project* adds,

> Toxic masculinity is a narrow and repressive description of manhood, designating manhood as defined by violence, sex, status and aggression. It's the cultural ideal of manliness, where strength is everything while emotions are a weakness; where sex and brutality are yardsticks by which men are measured, while supposedly "feminine traits"—which can range from emotional vulnerability

to simply not being hypersexual—are the means by which your status as "man" can be taken away.[15]

Clemens continues and capitulates that having discussions about toxic masculinity does not mean that men are

> bad or evil . . . NOT an assertion that men are naturally violent. . . . But in a culture that equates masculinity with physical power, some men and boys will invariably feel like they are failing at "being a man." For these particular men and boys, toxic masculinity has created a vacuum in their lives that can be filled through violence: through the abuse of women and of children in their care, through the affiliation with the so-called "alt-right" or ISIS, through gun violence of any other promise of restored agency that those parties wrongly equate with manhood.[16]

In connecting toxic masculinity and white male supremacy in culture, sociologist Kyle Kusz has written a soon-to-be-released book titled *Making American White Men Great Again: Tom Brady, Donald Trump, and the Allure of White Male Omnipotence in Post-Obama America*. Kusz asserts that the main reason for Brady's NFL popularity is "white rage and white supremacy."[17] Kusz also asserts that Brady and Trump are similar in that they surround themselves with white people.

Evidence of Brady's actions that illustrate his performance as a white male boils down to the fact that "he brings mostly white teammates"[18] to the Kentucky Derby each year. Likewise, his off-the-field friendships suggest "his performance of white masculinity shares much in common with President Trump's."[19] Trump's demonstration of white masculinity as president and Brady's performance are judged by the toxicity that is assumed as resident in skin color and actions taken as white males. Yet, when people of color exhibit similar masculine actions, no such masculinity is criticized, and no appropriation is assigned. The ultimate illustration for Kusz about Brady is based on the fact that "most of the Derby's attendees include white people."[20]

In an effort to combat what an increasing number of counselors and psychologists view as serious issues with maleness and masculinity, an innovative support group has been developed. One of the more recent Meetup.com groups has been established and goes by the name Men's Therapeutic Cuddle Group. The aim of the club is to redefine masculinity, according to Lehigh University's psychology professor Dr. Christopher Liang, who is also one of its supporters.[21]

Other such groups have been formed around the nation, which include (1) Cuddle Party, (2) Men Cuddling Men, (3) The Cuddle Network,

(4) Kuddles R Us, (5) The Kink Collective, (6) The Ecstatic Body, and (7) The Ecstatic Embrace.[22]

The organizers of the group state that the cuddling is non-sexual but also informs participants that sexual arousal does occur and it should be treated as a normal part of the experience from cuddling. Such groups are intended to help men to move beyond their limited and singular version of masculinity.[23]

According to recent trends, the American Psychological Association (APA) states "traditional masculinity is psychologically harmful. . . . socializing boys to suppress their emotions causes damage that echoes both inwardly and outwardly."[24] While no one would argue that emotions are good things to express, the notion that traditional masculinity should be suppressed and redefined simply misses the mark on several points.

First, demasculinizing males is no longer a pastime for far-left women's groups. There is a movement by today's gender warriors to remake men in their own image, and to do so beginning with male students. Essentially, there is a growing public shame in being a male and demonstrating masculinity. If the demonstration of masculinity is something *not liked*, then boys and men are in quick fashion labeled toxic or potential assaulters.

Second, boys and men are increasingly being told that they should apologize for their biology. This is terribly offensive to the mothers and fathers who raise their young men as they see fit. There is nothing toxic about their DNA and their birth biology. *Third*, the attack on masculinity is toxic in its own right. Not only does it marginalize, but it hurts human relationships. Boys at school may be fearful of addressing their teacher, complimenting a girl, or competing in a sport because one gender group deems these actions to be toxic in American culture.

In American culture today, there is a full-scale effort led by feminists and the LGBTQ+ lobbyists to shame men who are white, male, and evangelical. The movement to undermine is nothing new. However, it is much more concerted and being driven by a political wind during an election cycle. If masculinity were as toxic as claimed, why then would some transgenders and transsexuals seek transitions to such a toxic gender or sex?

Paul Nathanson and Katherine Young have written a trilogy on the current phenomenon. Two of these books are titled *Spreading Misandry*[25] and *Legalizing Misandry*.[26] The hatred of men and masculinism viewed from the perspective of feminists zeroes in on the twenty-first-century gender warriors. The main thesis is that men and masculinity are hated due to seeing the world through gynocentrism. Basically, the more that women make decisions for men and determine how they should and should not act, the more gynocentric the culture. In reality, the misandrism is as toxic to men as women claim masculinity is to them.

There is some pushback in culture. But notice that the blending of biological absolutes, the LGBTQ+ movement, the rise of radical misandry, and the feminization of young boys is leading to a resurgence of reexamining the *alpha male*,[27] which to some is another attempt to exercise toxic male dominance.[28] Mothers who push for their sons to exhibit their natural, biological and testosterone-driven competitive nature are marginalized by the current culture as being part of the problem.[29] Meanwhile, a mother pushing her son to take hormones to stop puberty is celebrated.

By and large, men's cuddle groups are geared for men whose views on masculinity are not traditional or whose experiences are laden with some form of trauma. Traditional masculinity is not evil. In addition to this, those whose gender identity have caused them distress or abuse directed toward them are more geared toward the need to understand their masculinity.

Certainly, cultural stereotypes within races, religions, genders, age groups, and a host of other distinct human demographics have work to do in understanding the roles of masculinity within their groups. However, to make the determination that there is one traditional masculinity that cuts across all of these demographics is to exercise a stereotype of its own and can be harmful for boys and their relationships with their fathers.[30]

Christopher Liang writes:

> There is a lot of diversity in the experience of men and masculinity, between groups, within groups and even within an individual. . . . What's important is to understand that despite all of this diversity, boys and men may experience incredible pressure to live up to these rules around masculinity that they may have learned within their own cultural context.[31]

Traditional masculinity is not expressed singularly, and any attempt to define masculinity as such does not take into consideration the vast range of males and how they view themselves.

Likewise, branding all traditional masculinity as harmful creates a toxic environment, especially when men already view themselves as emotional. Men bond with both men and women through athletics, various competitions, family events, weddings, funerals, reunions, when the nation is in need of military action, and in personal relationships. Men also bond with other men in accountability groups through churches and self-help groups. As men go, the number of ways they express emotions are countless. Efforts to fit masculinity into a theoretical box and treat it as a tinderbox waiting to express its toxicity is to diminish manhood at its core.

Studying women to understand men is not the best method to reach an understanding. Studying boys to understand girls is likewise a very weak strategy. Imagine studying white men to understand black men or studying Hispanics to better understand Asians? These approaches assume and presume that we are all quite the same. Clearly, people are not all the same.

The efforts to see people as one diminishes differences. "Once psychologists began studying the experiences of women through a gender lens, it became increasingly clear that the study of men needed the same gender-aware approach."[32] Essentially, men and women are viewed through gender lenses that are framed with preconceptions from modern psychological theories and supported by advocacy groups that lock down dissent.

Stating that traditional masculinity is harmful actually denigrates women whose vision and desire of masculinity is met in those of traditional male expressions. Expecting that men should be asking *for affection, asking for time, and asking other men for help* emotionally is just not how many men are wired. Teaching boys to do these very things in schools would be viewed by many parents as out of bounds. As long as men view cuddle groups as geared toward something meant for women and hear that sexual arousal occurs while hugging other men, traditional masculinity will view this attempt to redefine it as out of a social and masculinity engineering playbook.

In all fairness, if men are not allowed to step forward to have a voice with women's issues, under the notion that they do not understand women's bodies, their choices, and the issue of abortion, then it is quite fair to insist women refrain from asking questions that delve into the psyches and consciences of men. What do women know about a man's brain, their thoughts, their masculinity, their body and biology? These questions alone have built-in assumptions and lay the groundwork for debate. That being said, one person's debate is another person's toxic environment. Men are as different from women as masculinity is as different from femininity.

Educating the Whole Child

What does the whole child approach to education actually mean? The *Association for Supervision and Curriculum Development* (ASCD) considers educating the whole child in conjunction with Common Core State Standards. The organization defines the approach as

> policies, practices, and relationships that ensure each child, in each school, in each community is healthy, safe, engaged, supported, and challenged. . . .

> Within a whole child approach, questions must be raised about school culture and curriculum; instructional strategies and family engagement; critical thinking and social-emotional wellness. . . . The Common Core . . . is a critical step toward ensuring such a program.[33]

The reader does not have to delve too far into the platform of the whole child education paradigm to discover that its goal is not possible and for good reasons. The idea is connected to the failing Common Core holdover from the Obama administration. There is no consensus as to what it truly means. Others view whole child education from a different perspective.

According to Rana Hafiz, a veteran math teacher, "serving the whole child means 'supporting students in actually thinking about the world as a whole,' and figuring out how they can contribute to it."[34] Some consider teaching the whole child as a matter of social justice and that this fact should be taught across all subjects, whether it helps or hurts students. Others disagree. Regardless of the opinions, Seattle public schools are working to incorporate social justice into math curriculum.[35]

The fact that no one person or group really understands what whole child education really consists of is because it is a nebulous and intangible progressive ideology. The talking points appeal to parents in ways that sound like schools care for children as they do at home. The notion that any teacher, at any school, in any community could achieve this goal on any given day boggles the mind.

However, assuming such a reality could occur and each child in public school had his or her needs met over the course of a year, if the schools did not meet all of the children's spiritual needs—and apply truth in a spiritual sense to meet the faith or religious needs of children— the goal of educating the whole child would still be unmet. In short, meeting the needs of some children may become toxic to others due to the very nature that some students in some groups are given more attention than others. What should be said is schools meet the needs of some of the children in select groups, while others outside these groups do not receive the same attention.

A Missing Component

What is left out of today's whole child approach is a child's spiritual intelligence and his or her sense of right and wrong. These are usually extensions derived from their upbringing. And adding a student's faith into the mix brings even more scrutiny, but leaving it out means the philosophy in question must be renamed to meeting *almost all the needs of the almost whole child in almost educational and social ways.*

If a child demonstrates an interest in a fundamental belief and with this belief comes a deeply held spiritual worldview, what is a teacher to do? Would a teacher validate or negate the student's set of beliefs? Or how about an entire school forbidding parents to opt out of events that conflict with the spiritual home values of students and parents? Is this educating the whole child or focusing on select cultural fads of the day?

Adding the Spiritual?
An example of educating the whole child in contemporary society is best viewed in a story that occurred recently in the United Kingdom. "A mother in the United Kingdom has taken formal legal action against her son's former elementary school after he was not permitted to opt out of an event in celebration of Pride Month last June."[36] The parent was told that permission to opt out of the event was not granted because the event "related to the spiritual, moral, cultural, mental and physical development of pupils."[37] What is not being said to the parent was that it was counter to other students' spiritual, moral, cultural, mental, and physical development. To the school, the label of LGBTQ+ is perceived as spiritual as much as it is cultural and so, on its face, two opposite and competing spiritual views cannot be reconciled.

The school environment became toxic, and the parent said she felt that the odds were already stacked against her because the head teacher's daughter, who was present, was wearing a T-shirt that read, "Why be racist, sexist, homophobic, or transphobic when you could just be quiet?"[38] Forced attendance at rallies, marches, and gatherings such as these are not only happening in the United Kingdom. American students are being forced to listen to stories about alternate lifestyles in ways that, had the opposite viewpoint been shared as such, would be labeled hateful and toxic.

The truth is that the whole child approach comes with an agenda on the parts of those seeking to bring a generation into compliance with teachings that are in stark contrast to many students' family values. Yet, as long as there is no blowback, in-fighting, or major disagreements from parents, efforts to influence the culture of a generation will continue unabated. The influences upon students' emotions focus squarely on causing doubt by adding empathy and equity into the discourse. Therein lies the next phase to be discussed.

Schools Deciding for Children
Does educating the whole child mean that whatever adults deem important for children must be pressed into their minds and hearts? If so, apparently

there is nothing out of bounds in terms of curriculum and instruction, discipline, and restoration? If nothing is out of bounds, why then are school districts so unwilling to revisit and validate the historical Judeo-Christian values of our nation?

Political correctness has run amuck in public schools, and Americans know this. "Among the general population, a full 80 percent believe that political correctness is a problem in our country. Even young people are uncomfortable with it, including 74 percent ages 24 to 29, and 79 percent under age 24."[39]

Public schools are trying to do too much, with too little, for far too many and, in some cases, with misguided motives. This is a toxic disaster in the making. Teacher attrition is but one indicator of this toxicity. Parents pulling their children out of schools is another. The social agencies that schools have become are more like places of indoctrination than they are of education, and this should not be the purpose of schools or teachers.[40]

The fact is that parents understand there is no way to care comprehensively for the needs of their own children, let alone for the dozens in classrooms. Educating the whole child is impractical and impossible. Yet, all across this nation, with continued flagging results, teachers go about their business trying to fulfill an impossible goal. What could be more toxic to a career and people's lives than to work to exhaustion and illness toward something completely unattainable?

Just a quick analysis of time allocation reveals the impossibility of the approach. In classrooms of thirty students, how can teachers adequately allocate similar amounts of time to students if one-third to one-half are impoverished, cannot read because of learning disabilities, and are second language learners along with another one-third of the class at risk and with special needs and behavioral problems? In 2017–2018, "the number of students ages 3–21 who received special education services under the *Individuals with Disabilities Education Act* (IDEA) was 7.0 million, or 14 percent, of all public school students. Among students receiving special education services, 34 percent had specific learning disabilities."[41]

False optimism in the face of reality can actually produce a jaded view of teaching. For example, eyes roll when a district rolls out the newest and best-ever program aimed to help teachers teach and students learn. Veteran teachers have heard it all before. Educating the whole child is a great bumper sticker phrase, but, like all bumper stickers, they eventually fade from the fad they enticed and are eventually replaced. Meanwhile, the students come to them with greater and more severe issues, and some leave more frustrated than when they first arrived.

Social-Emotional Learning

The most recent program that is making headway in American schools is social-emotional learning. Observe the emphasis on embedding this program into student learning and the goals of focusing on social agency and emotional efficacy:

> For those unfamiliar, social emotional learning is defined by CASEL as "the process through which children and adults acquire and effectively apply the knowledge, attitudes, and skills necessary to understand and manage emotions, set and achieve goals, feel and show empathy for others, establish and maintain positive relationships, and make responsible decisions." CASEL has defined five core competencies it says should guide social emotional learning and are the five areas states will focus on while drafting their standards: self-awareness, self-management, social awareness, relationship skills, and responsible decision making.[42]

Social-emotional learning (SEL) is playing to mixed reviews. Some believe it to be one of the best programs ever to arrive in schools. To others, the program has proven to be toxic. One of the concerns of the program is people perceive its emphases as "all about psychologically and emotionally manipulating children in order to push a certain political agenda."[43]

Another concern comes by way of a connection to religious practice that has some parents upset. In 2012, the program MindUP, a social-emotional learning program trained students in Buddhist-style meditation. The program was supported by actress Goldie Hawn, who claimed one of its goals is to teach children "non-judgmental awareness of thoughts and feelings. . . . it actually teaches a child to judge any thought or feeling besides optimism and happiness as bad. It shows him how to escape the warnings of his conscience with pleasurable feelings—to make himself feel good even if he has done or experienced something that he ought to feel bad about."[44] For the record, Scientology and certain tenets of other American mind science religious groups have similar teachings.

That being said, the main concern about formative social-emotional learning programs are that they encourage children to do things for others with the incentive for achieving pleasurable sensations and dopamine highs.[45] Thus, "rather than practicing self-control, children instead practice self-indulgence. They learn to escape from reality and difficult relationships, rather than working through them."[46] This is what a growing number of Generation Z students are being taught in some schools. Do parents really wonder as to why some of their children have adopted a *me-first* notion of entitlement?⁴⁷

Rather than a teacher taking on a role to rear entitled children at school, Oleson and Wickelgren suggest "the way to help the child develop real self-control is tried and true: a caring adult patiently and unflaggingly commits to the moral training of that child. Directing, warning, correcting and disciplining day by day, hour by hour, moment by moment . . . the adult encourages the child to do what is right, whether or not it feels good. . . . There are no short cuts."⁴⁸

The Swiss philosopher Henri-Frederic Amiel (1821–1881) once said, "The test of every religious, political, or educational system is the [person] which it forms. If a system injures the intelligence it is bad. If it injures the character it is vicious. If it injures the conscience it is criminal."⁴⁹ Asking children to avoid standing on their principles and disagreeing where necessary is criminal and thereby toxic. According to Amiel, it is criminal.

Not everyone agrees with Olesen and Wickelgren in their assessment of MindUP. This is the case with Rebecca Calos, one of the proponents invested in the program. Calos writes:

> Through mindful practice, a child can become more aware of what might be causing pain or anxiety and therefore be better able to respond to this inner turmoil in a productive manner. A happy memory can help a child strengthen his resolve to overcome challenges and to move forward in a positive direction. Mindful awareness opens a child up to a world of possibilities. Children learn, in the MindUP program, the true meaning of optimism. Optimism is not rainbows and gold stars and sweet treats, but the belief that there *is* a solution. Optimists continue to struggle even against overwhelming odds because they are problem solvers and as such, their brains actively seek out new connections and possibilities. Optimists not only see the glass as half full, but as one that is continuing to be filled. The message that MindUP gives children: our world may present us with seemingly insurmountable problems, but through concentrated effort and a positive mindful awareness, together we can create a brilliant future.⁵⁰

The promises associated with unattainable goals do little to stress academics. Rather, these goals play on the natural imagination that comes in the character of children. SEL has taken hold in many states and has been labeled with *glowing terms*, such as the most comprehensive program to empower children, to *less stellar* reviews as the latest fad and to social engineering at its best.⁵¹

Supporters refer to the program as necessary for providing the tools for developing quality education. Detractors refer to the program as another government idea, using untrained teachers to address and manipulate the fragile nature of children.[52] For example, for the very first time, "states are allowed to define student success through non-academic factors that relate back to SEL. CASEL also applauds language that promotes 'safe and healthy students' in the process of supporting student achievement."[53]

A cadre of education experts

> believe that this increased support of things like SEL, character education and the like is a direct result of a "happiness enlightenment" . . . that for the first time . . . governments across the world are taking happiness seriously, realizing that happiness and well-being should be at the core of public policy because individuals and organizations are better, healthier and more productive when they are happy.[54]

Think about how this comes across to parents who battle their own inner addictions, those who lost a child to suicide, or the homeless families and the impoverished.

Parents should ask themselves why their own children at early ages begin to extol social and political beliefs that run counter to those of their upbringing. They should also ask why this is happening given that Common Core State Standards were supposed to be primarily about academics.[55]

Government Mandating Students' Feelings

Joy Pullman, of *The Federalist*, writes, "Here we have government demanding that young people exhibit certain feelings and social behaviors, and if they don't, their schools could be dinged for it. That's not only manipulative but creepy."[56]

Townhall journalist Jane Robbins states:

> Assessment and development of students' social and emotional skills is risky business. What kind of training will teachers or other school personnel have for this responsibility? . . . When non-psychologists dabble in these murky waters, the result is tremendously subjective analyses of what a child is thinking or feeling as opposed to what the government thinks he should be thinking or feeling. . . . SEL is nothing more than a big education fad that is destined to fail . . . a nonacademic version of Common Core.[57]

Robbins continues, "According to the monolithic progressive-education establishment in this country, SEL is the next big thing to fix the problems with public education. The same was true of outcome-based education, and Common Core, and fads infinitum. But this fad just isn't ineffective, it's dangerous. Parents should demand a halt to pseudo-psychology—and a restoration to their autonomy in raising their children,"[58] and schools should stick to academics in preparing students for the twenty-first-century economy.

Toxic Curriculum Choices

There is a fine line between curriculum that is controversial and curriculum that is toxic. Often, the best way to judge between the two is an analysis of the way curriculum is presented and whether the process is transparent. A second way to tell is the actual content, who teaches it, and to whom it is taught. During the age of NCLB, an example of a toxic school environment occurred over a book to be read by high school students.

In the early 2000s, a high school English and literature teacher was criticized for selecting a book by the late Toni Morrison, titled *The Bluest Eye*. Teachers, parents, school board members, and the district superintendent weighed in on the matter. Morrison's 1970 book contains dozens of expletives and a hefty dose of specific and graphic incestuous sex scenes.[59] The book had been labeled so graphic by its critics that they questioned whether 15-year-olds should be subjected to the language and depictions. That being said, the book earned a prestigious award, as did Morrison, eventually with the 1993 Nobel Prize in Literature.

Many of the opponents of the general usage of the book called for permission slips or better yet an optional book choice provided for those children and their parents whose values were in conflict with the teacher or author in question. The teacher had the authority to select the book for the class. There was another audience who wanted the book removed from the curriculum.

Advocates of the book maintained it was literature and that teenagers would glean life's lessons from understanding black culture of the era. Content meant less than the overall message since Morrison was a winner of many book awards. In fact, proponents of keeping the book began to refer to its critics as *book banners*. The district superintendent at the time was one of these critics who publicly referred to dissenting parents and teachers by the toxic term *book banners*.

Some teachers and parents sided with the superintendent and made clear that books like James Baldwin's *Go Tell It on the Mountain* had been read for years in schools. Others like Steinbeck's *The Grapes of Wrath*, Lee's *To Kill a Mockingbird*, Salinger's *Catcher in the Rye*, and Hugo's *Les Miserable* were standard texts in high schools.

There is vivid recollection of this controversy since this author had been asked to serve on a community-wide research and discussion panel regarding the book. The local newspaper sponsored the community panel. At the outset, the panel knew what it had been asked to do in offering its joint opinion on the matter. The panel was made up of a diverse set of parents and teachers from across the district.

The task of the panel was to read and analyze the book and make recommendations. The panel voted not to ban the book. We decided it best to limit use of the book to older students, those who would understand violent rape, molestation, sexual acts and incest, and its heavily graphic and violent sexual content. We questioned whether the book would lead to physical and emotional arousal as a result of its heavy sexual content.

The panel questioned why a teacher made the decision to select Morrison's book from the over two thousand books that were recommended by the state for secondary literature. It was a political decision made to counter parents' opinions. Dissenters were labeled toxic. The book's use was labeled as toxic curriculum. The superintendent was applauded for his stand as well as criticized as toxic for his approach. But the decision was made without really thinking through the contents of the book. Sometimes, principles can be toxic, especially absent facts.

Curriculum should be analyzed for its unintended consequences or recalling the ways previous students responded in class discussions. Reactions do not always equate to learning. Some who never read the book had no problem allowing other parents' children to read aloud and digest page after page of rape and incest culture. Parents should be encouraged to read Morrison's book and judge for themselves the quality of the literature and to be sure to ask themselves how students would feel when asked to read the F-bombs and hardcore porn–culture terms aloud in class. Parents should also apply this same privilege to every other aspect of their children's curriculum.

The lesson here is that schools have an obligation to gauge the pulse of their communities and engage the community for support. If they have to hide what they are doing with students, then this alone is enough to be accused of being toxic to some parents. Lack of transparency comes across as hiding something. This, in turn, violates trust and slips toward being toxic.

Triggers in Curriculum

If the same criteria were used today to decide on school curriculum, one would have to consider the triggers, offenses, and hurt feelings in the overall scheme of the decision. Children who come from sexual or physical abuse, who have gotten pregnant way too young, or who are victims of incest would react very differently today. Such triggers might be met with violence directly in the classroom.

Conversely, restricting a book from children might result in toxic accusations of misogyny, racism, or bigotry. Ironically, given today's social climate, if someone were to repeat Morrison's words as their own in social media posts, the words and the poster would be reported, and the account would be flagged for flagrant violations after warnings—even among adults.

Suggestions for Teachers in Avoiding Toxicity

It is always good to remember that, due to the nature of some of the issues that arise in schools, toxicity can never be completely avoided when working with the public. However, one of the most toxic classroom environments today involves the direct contrast between home values and school values over the teaching of gender identity and sexual attraction. The following seven suggestions are meant to assist teachers in thinking through how to reduce or avoid toxicity in the classrooms.

1. *Do not reduce students' religious beliefs to hateful opinions.* If the teacher dismisses students' beliefs to mere opinions, then the term *opinions* must be assigned to all others' beliefs as well. Beliefs relegated to opinions and labeled hateful when students disagree is toxic. If a teacher does not fairly apply the label of beliefs, then the teacher has taken sides and set in motion the beginning of a toxic learning environment. At this juncture, the teacher has lost some credibility by selecting which beliefs are legitimate ones.

If the teacher chooses to diminish all beliefs to mere opinions, some parents might view these actions as dismissive and undercutting of all students' beliefs. Therefore, acknowledging as valid all students beliefs is a way to avoid a toxic environment.

As an example, take the LGBTQ+-identified teacher who presents information that causes students to question their gender. Consider the learning environment if students hear the following:

> Gender is constructed through intergenerational experiences and social norms. Once we're aware of this, we can deconstruct the gender dichotomy and rebuild it as a fluid spectrum. . . . There are some simple ways to do this. Start saying "Good morning everyone," instead of saying "good morning boys and girls." Have critical conversations with your kids about the many assumptions we make based on gender, providing counterexamples, like boys who like to sing or girls who play sports. . . . I've even written gender out of the stories

I write with my class. In one instance, I was writing fairy tale adaptation of Cinderella for my class . . . using the pronoun *their* deliberately throughout.[60]

This approach becomes toxic to some parents and even some colleagues because it is based on subjective ideology and personal preference and comes with layers of agenda on the part of the teacher. It is also not based in science.

2. *Never shame a student by informing the student he or she is being misled and should get up to date with cultural trends.* Teachers must guard against focusing so much on issues of gender and sexuality, climate change, or any other social issues. Teachers need to avoid the appearance that their personal missions as educators are in the name of social justice or their own personal causes.[61]

Teachers err with the assumption that all students must be informed of the teachers' views and that the teachers' views comprise truth because of their identity. But, if permitted to do so, they must do so respectfully, which means being open to the latest science on the topic.[62] Education is not about the teacher, and the classroom is not the teacher's pulpit.[63] To assume anything else is to set up a toxic environment for those who disagree with the teacher's bias.

3. *Guard against dismissing dissenting students and telling them to go home and discuss the issues with their parents as a means to shut down classroom debate. Never accuse the students of needing to make certain that their family's beliefs should be corrected.* The teacher can control which issues are not addressed in the classroom and do so in dismissive fashion. This is not a good approach. Associated issues should be treated with the same integrity on the part of the teacher. If viewed otherwise, the teacher will be perceived as unfair and favorable only to those who agree with the teacher. This approach settles little and singles out the students who disagree. This has the tendency to set a toxic environment in motion.

4. *Teachers can seize moments to inform students that the class will be accepting of others' beliefs, personal expressions, and behaviors pertaining to any of their beliefs and no one should be ridiculed.* Take extra care with this type of classroom policy. If one student objects to something or shares a belief in contrast that causes a stir, the teacher's rule is then challenged. Disallowing the dissenting belief then results in a rule that has exceptions and is viewed as unfair. The primary problem with this approach is that the teacher sets the precedent that circumvented the very fairness expected from students. Secondly, the teacher's initial statement of tolerance comes across as intolerant disagreements that emerge, which then places students in toxic environments in which they are fearful of disagreeing.

5. *Teachers could state they are not going to address any issues controversial to students, their families, their schools, and communities.* This approach places the

teacher as arbiter, and one slipup brings the accusation of unfair. Bias creeps in and then begins to corrupt the environment where students then are waiting to catch the teacher in compromising inconsistencies.

For example, when teachers encourage students to question their own genders, sexual attraction, and various emotional connections as well as their spiritual teachings from home, they directly usurp parental responsibility and authority. This has become problematic to many parents because more and more teachers are being encouraged to utilize strategies "to foster a sense of inclusion for lesbian, gay, bisexual, transgender, and queer students"[64] and to assume that children naturally "come into . . . classrooms with a wealth of knowledge"[65] about matters of sex, gender, and biology and use them for the sake of shaping tolerance and understanding.

Toxicity may be produced when teachers view their jobs as conduits of progressive values and their mission as to "dismantle ways of thinking that reinforce the gender dichotomy and heteronormativity."[66] Toxicity may also be found in the creation of "safe spaces for children to explore their identities and empathize with those who are different from them."[67] Teachers must guard against stepping into the realms of parents because of their zeal to level the playing field on issues they deem important.

6. *Teachers must be careful when they ask students to embrace literature-based curriculum that embeds inclusion throughout.* By selecting literature specifically to target inclusion of one group, it may well produce an underlying level of anger on the part of some students and their parents. The use of curriculum as activism for one group may be both offensive and inappropriate. The test would be to run any such curriculum by the community and the parents of the students in the classroom. Educator Paul France argues for inclusion of LGBTQ+ identities in literature. He encourages teachers to:

> Include LGBTQ children's literature in your class library. As educators, we should provide both windows and mirrors in our curriculum, ensuring that our selection represents a diverse array of people and identities. This includes the LGBTQ community. While you may not know it yet—especially if you teach young children—there are students who will identify as LGBTQ at some point in their lives. Our job is to provide a safe space and role models for them as they age. This also means that we must represent the intersectionality that exists in the LGBTQ community, sharing stories of different genders, ethnicities, races, religions, and classes.[68]

The main problem here is that there is virtually no possibility that advocates of inclusion in literature would allow the presentation of dissenting scientific, psychological, and family counselors' views—much less the views of evangelicals for a literature balance. Most do not believe any such dissent is valid. A second problem is the assumption that all public school classrooms will have students who choose to identify with LGBTQ+ ideologies.

If this were flipped, evangelical Christian teachers bringing in literature in support of non-LGBTQ+ identities and such should have the same permission as would any others who use identities as justification for curriculum.

France makes some good points, but, with all ideologies that are unattainable, the practical biases usually win out. When this happens, a toxic environment is then created, and students lose in the process.

7. *Teachers can use dissent to their advantage since toxic environments exist in the real world and students need to learn to deal with these in their own ways.* The social agency aspect of caring for physical, mental, emotional, and social needs of children has become so very important. Culture and life experiences themselves have saddled some students and their teachers with highly personal toxic experiences that come to schools and express themselves, differently, each day.

Students need to get along and dissent with respect. They should never be forced to comply with others' beliefs and should never be forced to tolerate or accept them either. Rather, teachers would do well to demonstrate as adults how to show respect and disagree with character so that relationships with people can grow, even while not owning each other's differences. If students' identities are so very important, then why are schools adopting curriculum that seeks to shape and change dissent as well as celebrate only certain allowable identities? Are not all students' identities as important as those found within the current trend?

Effects of Toxic Teachings

Sometimes, good teachers take positions on issues in order to present many sides of the issues for students. But there are some issues today that are off-limits. In such cases, teachers align instruction for the sake of political correctness. Somewhere between the two, well-meaning teachers make mistakes. When they do, teachers should apologize to students and parents for their missteps.

Teachers who are toxic may sometimes be the edgy risk takers. Some might influence students to a pointed and one-sided perspective. This type of advocacy instruction does have its place and is what is expected today for issues of race, sex, gender, and several others. So disagreeing with anything in these categories through instruction can bring swift disdain and discipline toward a teacher. But limiting instruction to one side of issues limits students' education. One teacher learned a very difficult lesson while teaching his own history lesson on World War II.

A Bakersfield, California, high school history teacher flew an authentic Nazi flag in his classroom while teaching a unit on World War II and the Holocaust.[69] The teacher had flown the flag for nearly a decade at the same time of the year, with no complaints, until recently. Given the age in which teachers are accused of bias, he underestimated the immediate blowback from parents and students.

The teacher was pressured to take down the flag by incessant online shaming and threats. The rally cry was that, any time there is a symbol of hatred, there is an obligation to call it out and stand against it. According to several who complained, the teacher inadvertently offended groups of people and created a toxic environment. "According to Kern High School District spokeswoman Erin Briscoe, once the . . . [teacher] realized some students and parents were offended, he decided to take down the flag and refrain from displaying it in the future."[70]

Some in the local community were deeply offended that the flag was hanging in a public school classroom. Others thought it was appropriate given the subject matter. The issue to consider today, before any teacher instruction, is whether items deemed historical and authentic would now be viewed through a toxic lens, rather than an instructional aide.

Given the outcry, the flag itself was an element that became toxic, even though it was an artifact of historical significance. One of the most interesting parts of this story is that the teacher did not even stop to consider that people in today's generation might be offended by the flag. He somehow either missed or overlooked the shift in the emotional makeup of his students and their parents.

Teachers must remain culturally sensitive and literate to the changes that occur over the decades. Generation Z has a sense of entitlement that is exacerbated by their relationships with their smart devices,[71] and this ever so often interrupts education for the sake of social advocacy.

Another example of teachings accused of being toxic is found in a Houston-area teacher's lesson that was critical of President Trump.[72] The city's newspaper ran articles questioning the president's policies and implied he was against the paper's idea of American values by demonstrating insensitivity toward some racial and cultural groups. The junior high teacher in question asked whether Donald Trump should be president and asked students to relate whether Mexican Americans are the group seemingly targeted by the president's rhetoric and actions.[73]

Many parents and Texas politicians were deeply disturbed, and some were driven to anger over what they perceived as efforts to indoctrinate children to a political viewpoint. The school district chalked up the teacher's lesson to a *mistake*, saying that there was general agreement that the materials used for the lesson were not the best of sources. The official statement read, "the teacher make a simple error in judgment. Like all of us, teachers are human and make mistakes from time to time."[74]

What are toxic teachings doing to students in public schools and to the American culture in general? Quick observations of toxic teachings find that there are high levels of negative and positive emotions in classrooms with teachers who deliver toxic lessons. These emotions can sometimes be mistaken as *passion* or *excitement toward learning*. When teachers find their classrooms reach energy crescendos, they are encouraged to consider whether the effects are the direct cause of teacher instruction or whether students come to school with heightened sensitivities because of forces external to the classroom environment.

Students are sometimes harmed by instruction that directly hits their emotions—especially those with triggers that align with the content. The cognitive aspects of the lesson may be missed in favor of emotional reactions. Some students are surprised when teachers do not withhold opinions on issues for which the teachers feel strongly. In this age of immediate communications, teachers have no time to deescalate emotions or backtrack from a mistake in judgment. The immediacy of communications causes elevated attention with issues that would have dissipated in the past during the next instructional break. Toxicity can become an immediate factor in today's public school classrooms promoted by instructional methods by the teacher or by the content presented.

Why Unity on Some Issues Is Impossible

Thus far, it has been established that 100 percent academic proficiency in schools is impossible. Also established is that the goal of educating the whole child is also an impossible task. A third impossibility in education is unity on social and cultural issues.

As certain as one's religious views or political party affiliation, there are some issues upon which there will never be agreement. These are issues that are fixed or entrenched in the hearts and minds of people. Therefore, with issues such as abortion and same-sex marriage, immigration, the existence of God, health care, socialism, or capitalism and purposes of public education, a teacher must guard against his or her own personal biases entering the classroom.

There are certain issues on which there will always be a separation of opinion by parents of public school children. For example, the new sex education curriculum required to be taught in New Jersey and California requires a presentation of the history and accomplishments of those of LGBTQ+ orientations. Parents had very little to say in these decisions.

Today, sex education curriculum and books detailing LGBTQ lifestyles and sexual practices are being read by students in schools. Advocacy groups such as GLSEN,[75] PFLAG,[76] and GLAAD[77] are invited to school campuses periodically. In current American culture, LBGTQ+ issues remain toxic, despite political attempts to normalize in schools. Although the nation appears to be warming up to the normalization, literature and materials remain toxic to a large swath of the population. Again, parents had very little say in these decisions.

Opponents of the LGBTQ+ cultural push are labeled as intolerant, uneducated, homophobic, and haters. Frankly, opponents from both sides use these pejoratives—but that is because toxicity runs both directions and touches both sides of the political divide in the United States.

Parents are both in support of inclusion and normalization and also *not* in support of this shift in curriculum. For example, in protest of "Approved LGBT curriculum,"[78] California parents questioned "why do we need to know their orientation?"[79]

Others agreed with LGBT having the "same rights, but I don't when it's about teaching at school. There are hundreds of children from different backgrounds, so it's not appropriate."[80] Still others are a bit more caustic about what they perceive as forcing their children to become aware of a lifestyle and orientation of which they do not approve. Few issues today are more divisive for parents and children than those associated with sexuality and gender.

Even the role of the teacher is called into question. One parent writes, "Since when did sexuality ever need to be a teacher's job to teach a child?"[81] Whatever the case, there is a natural toxicity that surrounds some issues when children are involved, and this particular education issue remains one of them.

Are Your Lessons and Assessments Toxic?

How does one come to realize whether his or her teaching is toxic or whether it triggers some unknown aspects of trauma that lie dormant in a student's brain and emotions? Depending on the age group or grade level, this question takes on different levels of consideration and concern.

A sure way to bring forth the latest feelings that raise the levels of toxicity in schools is to be on the wrong side of student assessments today. If the classroom teacher is toxic and the curriculum is toxic, then what can be expected of assessments in line with these?

Standardized assessments have fallen into disfavor with teachers and parents nationally. "Unfortunately, standardized tests based on a narrowly prescribed curriculum and linked to specific grade levels are not a good way to judge student or teacher success."[82]

One can be sure that, if the results on the standardized assessments made both the teachers and students look good, there would be a different conclusion drawn. As it stands, an NEA survey of 1,500 teachers "found that while a majority of teachers did not think any of the state tests (i.e., PARCC, SBAC, and state-specific tests) were developmentally appropriate, there were statistically significant differences among the tests. Specifically, PARCC was seen as the least developmentally appropriate with Smarter Balanced and other state tests somewhat less so."[83]

Schools have become in large part social agencies, trying at every level to meet the needs of all students. The academic urgency of the past has now been replaced for social and emotional growth. The only problem is that state-level bureaucrats still expect to measure students academically, which frustrates "teachers in elementary and middle schools [who] were more likely to say the tests were not appropriate (77 and 75 percent respectively) while a smaller majority (58 percent) of high school teachers said they were not."[84]

Teacher comments posted at the conclusion of the NEA article are quite informative. One in particular sums up this chapter quite well. Regarding the toxic environment created by public education today, "Teachers always 'embrace' every stupid new mandate they cram down our throats. It's always swallow or choke."[85] Similarly, parents feel this same level of frustration when their children are forced to swallow values that are taught that are contrary to their upbringing.

Notes

1. Jane Robbins. "The latest big education fad, social-emotional learning, is as bad as it sounds." *Townhall.* August 8, 2016. Retrieved from https://townhall.com/columnists/janerobbins/2016/08/08/the-latest-big-education-fad-socialemotional-learning-is-as-bad-as-it-sounds-n2202205.

2. Staff. "Parents livid after middle school teacher hands out gender-identity graphic." *Yahoo News.* August 13, 2019. Retrieved from https://news.yahoo.com/parents-livid-after-middle-school-teacher-hands-out-genderidentity-graphic-204927365.html.

3. Deke Farow. "Denair school stops science teacher who was handing out 'gender unicorn' graphic." *The Modesto Bee*. August 19, 2019. Retrieved from https://www.modbee.com/news/local/education/article233676787.html?fbclid=IwAR3-hBJcApF0XRf3rHfs1rjKiTb3lRhyh6NVAdUqcNxIosuUpdBZxpwyzH4.

4. Ibid.

5. Ibid. Cf. *Trans Student Education Resources*. 2019. Retrieved from http://www.transstudent.org/.

6. Anna Brown. "Key findings on America's views of race in 2019." Pew Research Center. April 9, 2019. Retrieved from https://www.pewresearch.org/fact-tank/2019/04/09/key-findings-on-americans-views-of-race-in-2019/.

7. Robin DiAngelo. "White fragility." *International Journal of Critical Pedagogy*. 2011. 3(3): pp. 54–70. Retrieved from https://libjournal.uncg.edu/ijcp/article/viewFile/249/116.

8. Kelefa Sanneh. "The fight to redefine racism." *The New Yorker*. August 19, 2019. Retrieved from https://www.newyorker.com/magazine/2019/08/19/the-fight-to-redefine-racism.

9. Kelefa Sanneh. "The fight to redefine racism." *The New Yorker*. August 19, 2019. Retrieved from https://www.newyorker.com/magazine/2019/08/19/the-fight-to-redefine-racism.

10. Jeffrey C. Stewart. "Fighting racism even, and especially, where we don't realize it exists." *New York Times*. August 20, 2019. Retrieved from https://www.nytimes.com/2019/08/20/books/review/how-to-be-an-antiracist-ibram-x-kendi.html.

11. Tara C. Raines, Robyn Hess, Charles Barrett, et al. "Supporting marginalized students in stressful times: Tips for educators." *National Association of School Psychologists*. 2016. Retrieved from https://www.nasponline.org/resources-and-publications/resources-and-podcasts/diversity/social-justice/supporting-marginalized-students-in-stressful-times-tips-for-educators.

12. Colleen Clemens. "What we mean when we say, 'toxic masculinity.'" *Teaching Tolerance*. December 11, 2017. Retrieved from https://www.tolerance.org/magazine/what-we-mean-when-we-say-toxic-masculinity.

13. Ibid.

14. Ibid.

15. Ibid. Cf. Christopher Luu. "Meryl Streep doesn't agree with the term 'toxic masculinity.'" *Instyle*. May 31, 2019. Retrieved from https://www.instyle.com/news/meryl-streep-toxic-masculinity.

16. Colleen Clemens. "What we mean when we say, 'toxic masculinity.'"

17. Ryan Gaydos. "Tom Brady's popularity tied to rise in 'white rage and white supremacy,' professor says." *Fox News*. September 26, 2019. Retrieved from https://www.foxnews.com/sports/tom-brady-popularity-tied-white-supremacy?fbclid=IwAR3t6NDyxt7sUISzGnEoYLPJ9XdDqD_8ef17wXiw4DtIUL1nUMADMMCtLYI.

18. Ibid.

19. Ibid.

20. Ibid.

21. Staff. "Men's cuddling group aims to redefine masculinity and heal trauma." *Lehigh University College of Education.* March 26, 2019. Retrieved from https://ed.lehigh.edu/news-events/news/men%E2%80%99s-cuddling-group-aims-redefine-masculinity-and-heal-trauma.

22. "Meetups." Retrieved from https://www.meetup.com/find/?allMeetups=false&keywords=Me%27s+Therapeutic+Cuddle+Group&radius=Infinity&userFreeform=Seattle&mcId=c98101&change=yes&sort=default.

23. Aneri Pattani. "Men's cuddling group aims to redefine masculinity and heal trauma." *Philadelphia Inquirer.* March 25, 2019. Retrieved from https://www.inquirer.com/health/men-cuddling-group-healing-trauma-mental-health-20190325.html.

24. Stephanie Pappas. "APA issues first-ever guidelines for practice with men and boys." *American Psychological Association.* Vol. 50(1): 34. Retrieved from https://www.apa.org/monitor/2019/01/ce-corner.

25. Paul Nathanson and Katherine Young. *Spreading misandry: The teaching of contempt for men in popular culture.* 2006. London, England: McGill-Queen's University Press.

26. Paul Nathanson and Katherine Young. *Legalizing misandry: From public shame to systemic discrimination against men.* 2006. London, England: McGill-Queen's University Press.

27. Staff. "Top 5 traits of a confident alpha male." *Manscaped.* October 2, 2018. Retrieved from https://www.manscaped.com/blogs/style/top-5-traits-of-a-confident-alpha-male.

28. Rachel Hosie. "The myth of the alpha male." *Independent.* May 9, 2017. Retrieved from https://www.independent.co.uk/life-style/the-myth-of-the-alpha-male-a7724971.html.

29. Joanna Schroeder. "8 things you must never do when raising boys." *Good Men Project.* July 28, 2017. Retrieved from https://goodmenproject.com/featured-content/things-you-must-not-do-when-raising-boys-hesaid/.

30. Ibid.

31. Stephanie Pappas. "APA issues first-ever guidelines for practice with men and boys."

32. Ibid.

33. Staff. "A whole child approach to education and the Common Core State Standards Initiative." Association for Supervision and Curriculum Development. No date. Retrieved from http://www.ascd.org/ASCD/pdf/siteASCD/policy/CCSS-and-Whole-Child-one-pager.pdf.

34. Rachel Burstein. "Educators don't agree on what whole child education means. Here's why it matters." *EdSurge.* July 16, 2019. Retrieved from https://www.edsurge.com/news/2019-07-16-educators-don-t-agree-on-what-whole-child-education-means-here-s-why-it-matters.

35. Katherine Timpf. "Seattle public schools want to teach social justice in math class. That hurts minorities." *National Review.* October 22, 2019. Retrieved from https://

www.nationalreview.com/2019/10/seattle-public-schools-proposal-teach-social-justice-in-math-class/.

36. Heather Clark. "UK mother takes legal action against primary school for not allowing son to opt out of gay pride event." *Christian News*. March 26, 2019. Retrieved from https://christiannews.net/2019/03/26/uk-mother-takes-legal-action-against-primary-school-for-not-allowing-son-to-opt-out-of-gay-pride-event/?fbclid=IwAR3y1LcEYxUK-VY7znIuncouGPgLM4q60N31Omjvagby4S7ajednmXF53wk.

37. Ibid.

38. Ibid.

39. Yascha Mounk. "Americans strongly dislike PC culture." *Atlantic*. October 10. 2018. Retrieved from https://www.theatlantic.com/ideas/archive/2018/10/large-majorities-dislike-political-correctness/572581/.

40. Zachary Wright. "It's non-negotiable. We have to teach social justice in our schools." *Education Post*. December 4, 2017. Retrieved from https://educationpost.org/its-non-negotiable-we-have-to-teach-social-justice-in-our-schools/.

41. Staff. "The condition of education." National Center for Education Statistics. May 2019. Retrieved from https://nces.ed.gov/programs/coe/indicator_cgg.asp.

42. Nicole Gorman. "Critics of social emotional learning standards call it a fad, 'non-academic Common Core.'" *Education World*. August 8, 2016. Retrieved from https://www.educationworld.com/a_news/critics-social-emotional-learning-standards-call-it-fad-non-academic-common-core-498184814.

43. Nicole Gorman. "Critics of social emotional learning standards call it a fad, 'non-academic Common Core.'" Cf. Joy Pullman. "Tennessee to create safe spaces in k–12 schools." *The Federalist*. August 8. 2016. Retrieved from https://thefederalist.com/2016/08/08/tennessee-to-create-safe-spaces-in-k-12-schools/#disqus_thread.

44. Tina Olesen in Ingrid Wickelgren. "How social and emotional learning could harm our kids." *Scientific American*. November 27, 2012. Retrieved from https://blogs.scientificamerican.com/streams-of-consciousness/how-social-emotional-learning-could-harm-our-kids/.

45. Ibid.

46. Ibid.

47. Ernest J. Zarra III. *The entitled generation*. 2017. Lanham, Maryland: Rowman & Littlefield Publishers.

48. Tina Olesen in Ingrid Wickelgren. "How social and emotional learning could harm our kids."

49. Henri-Frederic Amiel. "Quotes on government, governing, politicians and politics." *Journal*. June 17, 1852. Retrieved from https://tentmaker.org/Quotes/government_and_governing_quotes8.htm.

50. Rebecca Calos in Ingrid Wickelgren. "Social and emotional learning empowers children." *Scientific American*. November 27, 2012. Retrieved from https://blogs.scientificamerican.com/streams-of-consciousness/social-and-emotional-learning-empowers-children/.

51. Jane Robbins. "The latest big education fad, social-emotional learning, is as bad as it sounds." *Townhall*. August 8, 2016. Retrieved from https://townhall.com/columnists/janerobbins/2016/08/08/the-latest-big-education-fad-socialemotional-learning-is-as-bad-as-it-sounds-n2202205.

52. Ibid.

53. Nicole Gorman. "Critics of social emotional learning standards call it a fad, 'non-academic Common Core.'"

54. Ibid.

55. Perry Chiaramonte. "Common Core lessons blasted for sneaking politics into elementary classrooms." *Fox News*. January 12, 2017. Retrieved from https://www.foxnews.com/us/common-core-lessons-blasted-for-sneaking-politics-into-elementary-classrooms.

56. Joy Pullman. "Tennessee to create safe spaces in K–12 schools." *The Federalist*. August 8, 2016. Retrieved from https://thefederalist.com/2016/08/08/tennessee-to-create-safe-spaces-in-k-12-schools/#disqus_thread.

57. Jane Robbins. "The latest big education fad, social-emotional learning, is as bad as it sounds."

58. Ibid.

59. Toni Morrison. *The bluest eye*. 2007. New York: Penguin-Random House Publishers.

60. Paul France. "Supporting LGBTQ students in elementary school." *Edutopia*. May 31, 2019. Retrieved from https://www.edutopia.org/article/supporting-lgbtq-students-elementary-school.

61. Brittney Beck. "We must nurture youth activism in Kern." *The Bakersfield Californian*. September 14, 2019. Retrieved from https://www.bakersfield.com/opinion/community-voices-we-must-nurture-youth-activism-in-kern/article_e9b53224-de36-11e9-9e80-a729715eaeb0.html.

62. Andrea Ganna, Karin J. H Verweij, Michel G. Nivard, et al. "Large scale GWAS reveals insights into the genetic architecture of same-sex sexual behavior." *Science*. August 30, 2019. Vol. 365. Retrieved from https://science.sciencemag.org/content/sci/365/6456/eaat7693.full.pdf. Cf. Robert Verbruggen. "Death of the 'Gay Gene.'" *National Review*. September 3, 2019. Retrieved from https://www.nationalreview.com/2019/09/death-of-the-gay-gene/.

63. Paul France. "Supporting LGBTQ students in elementary school." *Edutopia*. May 31, 2019. Retrieved from https://www.edutopia.org/article/supporting-lgbtq-students-elementary-school.

64. Ibid.

65. Ibid.

66. Ibid.

67. Ibid.

68. Ibid.

69. Steven Mayer. "Nazi flag taken down in classroom at Frontier High School." *The Bakersfield Californian*. February 1, 2019. Retrieved from https://www

.bakersfield.com/news/nazi-flag-taken-down-in-classroom-at-frontier-high-school/article_a8c4aaa8-2651-11e9-9729-6fbb65c1fb77.html.

70. Ibid.

71. Ernest J. Zarra III. *The entitled generation*, pp. 93–112.

72. Louis Casiano. "Trump-related school assignment prompts anger, death threats against Houston-area teacher: Report." *Fox News*. March 28, 2019. Retrieved from https://www.foxnews.com/us/trump-related-assignment-prompts-anger-death-threats-against-houston-area-teacher.

73. Ibid.

74. Ibid.

75. Gay, Lesbian, Straight Education Network (GLSEN). Retrieved from https://www.glsen.org/.

76. Parents, Families and Friends of Lesbians and Gays. (PFLAG). Retrieved from https://pflag.org/.

77. Gay and Lesbian Alliance Against Defamation (GLAAD). Retrieved from https://www.glaad.org/.

78. Marlei Martinez. "Curriculum change prompts parent sit-out at Rocklin schools." *KCRA News*. May 2, 2019. Retrieved from https://www.kcra.com/article/lgbtq-curriculum-inclusion-parent-sit-out-rocklin-schools/27351319.

79. Marlei Martinez. "Curriculum change prompts parent sit-out at Rocklin schools." Cf. Staff. "Parents protest approved LGBT curriculum by keeping children out of school." *Yahoo News*. May 6, 2019. Retrieved from https://news.yahoo.com/parents-protest-approved-lgbt-curriculum-171359732.html.

80. Ibid.

81. Marlei Martinez. "Curriculum change prompts parent sit-out at Rocklin schools." KCRA News

82. Tim Walker. "Survey: 70 percent of educators say state assessments not developmentally appropriate." *NEA Today*. February 18, 2016. Retrieved from http://neatoday.org/2016/02/18/standardized-tests-not-developmentally-appropriate/.

83. Ibid.

84. Ibid.

85. Ibid.

CHAPTER SIX

Detoxing American Schools

> When I started teaching, I was excited to make an impact on children. I loved every minute of my job. . . . I am leaving the field of education. I have had so many wonderful memories. But it has become a toxic profession.
>
> —Jonathan Carroll[1]

When humans are working together closely, professional and personal relationships develop. Some of these relationships are based on work alone, while others extend beyond the places of employment. New teachers who are hired go through a cultural adjustment period. However, a school's culture is experienced quickly by almost everyone who steps onto the campus, whether as employees, parents, or students. But what are these people actually sensing about school culture?

Undeniably, school culture is best experienced by those who spend time within its culture. School culture "is often invisible . . . and it can be one of the most important components of what makes a school great."[2] School culture can affect observers in a very short period of time. What does personally experiencing school culture accomplish toward understanding the nature of toxicity that might exist on a school campus?

Toxic Schools

Life and nature are full of toxins.

Nature, it turns out, is one big medicine cabinet. We can thank the willow plant for the salicin that turned into aspirin, and the poppy for the pain-killing powers of morphine. Even poison can become potions—a viper's venom, for instance, is part of a powerful anti-clotting drug that can keep blood flowing instead of clumping up. . . . From cancer treatments to painkillers . . . agents that may be hazardous materials today but could evolve into powerful medicines tomorrow.[3]

The obvious question then is, since toxins are part of the natural course of life, can they be used for good where they appear as catalysts between people? In other words, for teachers and schools, can a recognized workplace toxin ultimately be used for good? The obvious answer is yes, but it takes those with more of an optimistic outlook on life to see this through toxicity and into the possibility.

Since optimism runs counter to most school toxicity, the optimist has to work hard to bring others along. Schools, like science laboratories, can be full of toxicity. But the problem is there are no jars, and labeling is just not necessarily helpful.

Researchers are working through how best to define and describe toxic schools. Kent Peterson in the *Journal of Staff Development* states that toxic schools have an overall negative feel and that toxic schools

- lack a clear sense of purpose,
- have norms that reinforce inertia,
- blame students for lack of progress,
- discourage collaboration, and
- often have actively hostile relations among staff.[4]

There is no surprise then that toxic schools begin with negative culture. When this culture becomes contagious, schools become quite messy.

Characteristics of a Toxic School

A toxic school can be characterized by a number of indicators. Stephany Soto suggests the following ten for starters.[5] Check these and others against your experience, by using the checklist in table 6.1 to determine whether there is the possibility that your school culture is toxic.

Soto zeroes in on the toxicity that develops among teachers and administrators throughout a given year. If schools truly want to detoxify their faculty and students, then the obvious first step is to take the suggestions from Soto

Table 6.1. Is Your School Toxic?

Indicator	Yes	No	Uncertain
1. Teachers do not trust the majority of their colleagues with private or even public information.			
2. Teachers and parents cannot trust the administrator or principal to be consistent.			
3. Teachers with energy and good ideas find it difficult to break through cliques supported by faculty.			
4. Select teachers are naysayers and have become embittered, speaking negatively of even the smallest of school issues.			
5. Teachers gripe about how much time is wasted on things that are not related to teaching and learning.			
6. Teachers' personalities have become numb to their loved ones and sometimes demonstrate short-tempered dispositions because of physical and mental exhaustion.			
7. Teachers feel unsafe in being able to share freely with others and feel like they have to continue to look over their shoulders.			
8. Teachers begin to break down physically and emotionally because of stress.			
9. Teachers experience more and more moments of loss of patience and even have thoughts of doing something extreme so as not to have to go to work.			
10. Teachers are missing more and more school days for illnesses.			

and others and begin remediating the school program in small steps. Schools that focus on teaching and learning are amazing places to visit. Teachers doing what they are trained to do yield amazing results. Distractions to these purposes tend to move education incrementally away from academics.

Along with the high expectations of student achievement, teachers today are pressured with more extraneous and added responsibilities. As pressures mount, teachers and administrators begin to run on empty. The effects on students yield negative returns, and everyone included becomes a victim of the system. Part of any toxic school environment is attributed to the education system itself.

Drilling down into toxic schools, it does not take long to find teachers who have become disillusioned and jaded. The Internet abounds with stories about teachers who had enough of working in schools. So they walk away from the toxicity and, in so doing, leave their passion to teach behind. Jonathan Carroll is an example of the scores of teachers sharing their personal stories.

> I think of all the things I did not sign up for . . . like micromanaging administrators, mental health counseling, blueprints with no freedom or flexibility . . . not being considered an expert in my chosen field even though I have a graduate degree. Students overdosing on drugs and collapsing in my classroom when they get back from the bathroom. Active shooter drills. Teachers being armed. Knowing where it is safe to hide in my classroom. Feeding and clothing my students. Buying my own supplies. Being told I should be thankful I have a job and to get over myself. I am tired of the constant testing . . . tired of everyone else knowing better and being chastised if I dare ask questions or challenge leadership. So . . . I am walking away.[6]

Carroll's frustrations capture the essence of what today's schools have become. They have lost their academic urgency, and many are now systemically scattered into social agencies. So many elements and tasks have been added to schools that teaching and learning are less important than social issues. Directly in the center of all of this frustration is the expectation of assessments.

It is Carroll's experience that "intense standardized testing makes children burn out and teachers anxious over whether their classroom scores will impact their employment. Those tests . . . don't measure much."[7] Although the tests don't measure much, they take measurable and precious time away from student learning to prepare for them. Assessment culture can become toxic very quickly, as veteran teachers found under No Child Left Behind. But the system of assessments in states has not breathed its last, just yet.

Assessment Burnout

In Florida, the English Language Arts state assessments became so toxic that some parents opted to withhold their children from taking them.

> Some third-graders—including honors students—from a number of school districts were denied promotion because they opted out of the test. The parents of these students, who are part of a national testing opt-out movement, went to court and sued their districts. . . . The 1st District Court of Appeals [ruled]

> ... The purpose of the ELA is to assess whether the student has a reading deficiency and needs additional reading instruction before (and after) being promoted to fourth grade. ... The test can only achieve that laudable purpose if the student meaningfully takes part in the test by attempting to answer all of its questions to the best of the student's ability. Anything less is a disservice to the student—and the public.[8]

However, here is where the 1st District Court of Appeals decision became toxic. Its ruling "ignored years of research that shows that high-stakes standardized test scores are not reliable or valid, and it ignored the problems Florida has had with its standardized testing accountability system, which became so severe that school superintendents statewide revolted in 2015 and said they had 'lost confidence' in its accuracy."[9]

Teachers complained about the state's imbalanced focus on assessments and related their own complaints to the state. The toxic environment around assessments has resulted in the following conclusions that assessments

> (1) Are unavoidably biased by social-class, ethnic, regional, and other cultural differences. (2) Unfairly advantage those who can afford test prep. (3) Radically limit teacher ability to adapt to learner differences. (4) Penalize test-takers who think in nonstandard ways. (5) Emphasize minimum achievement to the neglect of maximum performance. (6) Create unnecessary stress and negative attitudes toward schooling. (7) Channel increasing amounts of tax money away from classrooms and into corporate coffers. (8) Subtract from available instructional time. (9) Create test fatigue, aversion, and eventual refusal to take tests seriously. (10) Undermine a fundamental democratic principle that those closest to the work are best positioned to evaluate its quality.[10]

Schools are toxic when they are imbalanced and focus on one element of education to the exclusion of many of the other important elements in educational learning. Similar results occur when schools focus on one demographic and lessen the attention on others. These unintended consequences result in toxic school environments. Elected officials ought to know better.

Full-Plated Teacher Stress
If people are serious about detoxing public schools, states and districts should stop adding more and more each year to the plates of teachers. In toxic schools, teacher stress levels are off the charts. Herman, Reinke, and Hickman-Rosa published a study on teacher stress levels. They determined that "93 percent of elementary school teachers report that they are experiencing a high stress level."[11]

Students were also included in their study. Overall, the

participants in this study were 121 teachers and 1,817 students in grades kindergarten to fourth from nine elementary schools in an urban Midwestern school district. Latent profile analysis was used to determine patterns of teacher adjustment in relation to stress, coping, efficacy, and burnout. . . . Three classes were characterized by high levels of stress and were distinguished by variations in coping and burnout ranging from (a) high coping/low burnout (60%) to (b) moderate coping and burnout (30%), to (c) low coping/high burnout (3%). The fourth class was distinguished by low stress, high coping, and low burnout. Only 7% of the sample fell into this Well-Adjusted class. Teachers in the high stress, high burnout, and low coping class were associated with the poorest student outcomes.[12]

The data indicate that toxic environments and extreme stress levels are highly correlated. Both can lead to burnout of teachers and students. In recognition of this toxicity, *teacher burnout* is now an official medical diagnosis, according to the World Health Organization.[13] Administrators can help alleviate some of the stress, but they are under immense pressures of their own. In any case, administrators can set the tone in their building for how teachers are perceived and supported.

"Prioritizing teacher well-being and giving higher rates of recognition and feedback to teachers versus criticism and judgment helps set a positive tone."[14] Teacher burnout and teacher attrition are results of factors such as physical exhaustion to unreal expectations. These are also directly related to teachers unable to spend time exercising their passion, which is to teach.

When school administrators fall short of empathy or are insensitive to what their teachers face each day, teachers often wonder whether they are truly supported. Some wonder if they are even recognized day to day for their efforts. These feelings add to the toxicity of the workplace. No teacher is meant to be an island. What teachers on edge should never hear out of the mouths of pressured administrators is the statement, "Well, you asked for this job."[15] Toxic responses only worsen school environments and ultimately affect children in the classroom.

Administrator Empathy

One of the more important comments made by teachers with respect to administrators is that teachers long for their superiors to have had significant time as teachers before becoming administrators. There seem to be different levels of empathy with the veteran teacher who becomes an administrator compared to the fast-tracked lesser-experienced administrator—especially when it comes to evaluating teachers. Districts and schools that focus on hiring from within a certain demographic, over others who are better qualified only because of issues of justice or by another politically motivated decision, are not helping to reduce toxicity within the system.

Evaluating teachers, whether formally or informally, and "focusing on how educators succeed or fail at 'coping' with job pressures can be misconstrued as placing the blame squarely on those individuals. Talking too much about 'burnout,' for example, implies that many teachers simply can't hack it in the classroom and it's ultimately up to them to make the necessary changes."[16] Administrator empathy increases because of lengthy educational experiences. These experiences can provide an understanding of the new age of education, its current cultural shift, and the delicate mix of the natures of twenty-first-century parents, students, and teachers whose lives are immersed in emotion, identities, and smart technologies.

There is some truth to the statement that what teachers focus on will be where their energies are placed. Also true is what teachers are forced to focus on may not receive the most energetic of instructional responses. Numerous factors require the attention of teachers with things not relevant to teaching and yet come at them at a furious pace. "The stress level felt by educators is a wake-up call to the country about the state of the profession, but supporting their use of effective coping strategies must be part of the solution—and educators recognize this."[17] As a result, as Tim Walker asserts, "Everyone knows that teaching is one of the most demanding and stressful professions. And most are probably aware that a majority of teachers are feeling a high level of stress."[18] When stress comes as a result of a change in basic sensibilities or even from a shift in societal norms, some of the first to experience the pressure of these changes are the teachers.

Are Boys and Girls the Same?

In twenty-first-century American public schools, the assault on traditional norms has become insistent. Traditional American values are being revised, rewritten, and even discarded. Along with new ideas on race, sex, and gender comes another progressive proposition that masculine American men and boys are now associated with what is called *toxic masculinity*.

Colleen Clemens explains:

> Boys will be boys . . . when we unpack this comment, we see that it perpetuates negative ideas about what we expect from our boys, particularly when it comes to aggression. First, the phrase implies that boys are biologically wired

to be violent, rough and tumble—and that they should be excused from any consequences for that behavior. When our culture buys into the idea that the "male sex" (not gender) is hardwired for violence, we can excuse behaviors that hurt others physically and emotionally.[19]

The 1990s ideas of gender differences have been tossed aside, and this discarding has greatly impacted a generation of teachers and teacher education institutions. Essentially, what is being said today is that boys' and girls' brains are the same and the way people feel makes them who they are.

In contrast to the fads of the 1990s, which drew many clear lines of distinction between males and females, Clemens asserts the newest view. She explains:

> Despite what '90s self-help books may say, when discussing sex (not gender), men are not from Mars, and women aren't from Venus. Neuroscientist Lise Eliot has done extensive work to show that the brains of girls and boys are not all that different. Such biological essentialism argues that "boys will be boys" because their biology naturally leans toward violence and aggression. When such a belief is upheld in a classroom, it contributes to a toxic foundation to boys' senses of self. How people identify allows us to define gender differently. If we think about gender as distinct from sex, as the way someone feels as opposed to something that is biological, we can no longer excuse negative behaviors in or out of the classroom with the line, "Boys will be boys."[20]

In other words, under the assumption that girls and boys brains are essentially the same, why is it that boys are the ones exhibiting such toxic and violent behaviors? Shouldn't the girls also be exhibiting something similar? Clemens admits that "Toxic masculinity relies on notions."[21] One of these ideas is that "boys are incapable of expressing themselves through means other than violence. . . . To girls, the message is, 'that violent act to which you did not consent means that he feels love for you.' And the message to boys is, 'When you feel an emotion, you should express it through violence.'"[22]

Based on Clemens's notions, she then extrapolates the following:

> This kind of thinking implies that it's strange for boys to have feelings of love that are disconnected from feelings of violence. . . . When we tell our boys it's normal to show that they like someone by hurting them, we don't just excuse toxic masculinity—we encourage it. We are effectively not teaching our children what safe and consensual relationships look like at the moments when they are just starting to come of age sexually.[23]

Schools that proactively instruct boys to be other than who and what they are biologically and naturally are seeking to reengineer male identities.

From the perspective of many parents, the very idea that schools would attempt such things is evidence of toxicity. For example, traditionalist men and women would view this as an attempt to feminize their masculine boys and understand it as highly toxic.

In a final assertion by Clemens, she explains:

> I respect the boys and men in my life too much to have such low expectations for them. Their biology does not demand that they become assaulters. And their biology does not necessitate that they speak about women in vulgar ways. Our constructed beliefs about masculinity teach them that, in order to "man up," they must perform their masculinity in aggressive ways—or have their masculinity questioned.[24]

Clemens equates her ideas to higher expectations and draws a toxic conclusion. She implies that all boys reared by discipline-oriented fathers, highly competitive athletes, or military men are ticking time bombs whose fuses are lit by a social construct they believe exists.

What could be more insulting and elitist than the idea that boys are potentially toxic and that teachers must guide boys into parts of their emotions in order to relax and subdue them?

While the recent fad is to diminish masculinity as we know it, the other half of the equation is left unattended. The implication is that girls are not toxic like masculine boys. This is simply not the case. The danger of this current trend of toxic masculinity is that any boy who disagrees with a teacher or something being taught or even takes a bold stand for a deeply held personal belief could come away with a label placed on him. It must also be assumed when dealing with fathers.

Which teacher or school has the right to step in and admonish parents because of the assumption that a certain expression of masculinity is somehow a force for a boy's toxic behavior in class? Boys are indeed different from girls in more ways than they are similar. The starting point of neuroscience provides excellent evidence to support this conclusion.

There is the cultural assumption that patriarchal and male-dominated cultures produce toxic males. But what happens when girls and women are just as toxic? Certainly, the general consensus is that toxic children come from toxic parents pushing their children into toxic environments with expectations placed upon them.[25] The time may come when it is plausible that some of the teachings on gender may lead to unintended expressions of toxicity of their own.

There is an impact of toxicity upon females that is leading to an increase of violence and physical fights and bullying in schools—particularly in inner cities.²⁶ Our culture now celebrates women who physically beat each other up in competition. If men are accused of being toxic and violent in competition and across all sectors of culture, then why does this same culture accept and promote women to be the same as men? Are men and women the same? Is toxic masculinity a trait in women, or are they toxic as females and being merely affected by a masculine construct? Humans have tendencies to be toxic, and most often gender has absolutely nothing to do with its expression.

There is irony in many things pertaining to the issues surrounding toxicity. For example, the push to detox our nation's schools, demasculinize males, and equalize genders apart from biology is brought together in California's new ban on school suspensions and expulsions. With the focus on toxicity of males, progressives think that restricting disciplinary action to those who commit only violent offenses would detox school environments. Just the reverse has happened.

Anti-discipline advocates claim that suspensions can be replaced by *restorative justice* and *healing circles*. In reality, that does further damage. A gold-standard study from the RAND Corporation found that, in Pittsburgh, restorative justice harmed academic achievement among black students.

Anti-discipline advocates claim that they are fighting the school-to-prison pipeline. In reality, their policies increase the flow. The idea that not holding kids accountable for their actions will make them more law-abiding as adults is idiotic. If we tell juveniles there are no consequences for misbehavior, we set them up for failure in the workplace. And we put them at risk for a hard reckoning when they find that behavior that didn't even get them suspended in school gets them a felony charge when they hit age 18.

For additional evidence, look no further than Los Angeles. When the school board banned suspensions, referrals to law enforcement increased 145 percent. And, in 2018, threats of violence in Los Angeles schools increased by 70 percent.²⁷

Could this result not be foreseen when schools place social agency over academics and social justice over safety? It is high time to refocus our schools on academics and leave behind the social engineering meant to remake culture in the image of one political group or another.

Toxicity Is Not Just an American Problem

Each night when school is over teachers all over the world leave their campuses and head to their homes. In the United Kingdom, some teachers are "leaving school in groups because they are scared of vicious attacks from parents." "The National Association of Head Teachers (NAHT) has warned that both violent and physical attacks from parents and pupils are 'increasing in both severity and regularity,'"[28] and not all of these attacks are from males.

Camilla Turner explains: "Head-teachers also complained about the threats and abuse they receive online, via social media, which can damage their reputation. Earlier this week, the Education Secretary said that teachers need protection from 'vitriolic' online abuse."[29] Since data indicate women are more likely to use platforms of social media and use them more often than men,[30] it does raise the question as to why some of these female parents are so toxic. Even as attention is "mainly focused on protecting young people from possible online danger, they are by no means the only victims. The internet is not selective and I know that teachers and leaders can be vulnerable too."[31] Nations around the world are reporting upswings in violence against teachers.[32] It is doubtful that a Westernized view of masculinity is the cause of this violence since it cuts across all boundaries, races, ethnicities, and religions. Whether American sophisticates will admit it or not, there is something toxic and endemic to the nature of humans. Such toxicity cannot be engineered out by the newest of fads that make their way down the stairs of ivory towers.

Questions for Further Research

The following list includes additional questions on toxic masculinity that need further research.

- Do girls really want boys to be more like girls given that the ideas of toxic masculinity imply there are similarities in the brains of boys and girls?
- Should single mothers be blamed for their sons who grow up to demonstrate toxic masculinity?
- Where is the science that verifies all the notions, suggestions, and ideas of toxicity resident within boys and men?
- What positive aspects does toxic masculinity have to offer American culture?
- Does sexually objectifying girls and women play any part in drawing out toxicity among boys and men?
- In what ways would men becoming less toxic affect the military and their involvement in warfare?
- Are girls and women in athletics being trained to demonstrate a toxic masculinity or toxic femininity, or is there no distinction because of claimed brain similarities?

- Is social media and ganging up against others in order to shame an example of toxic masculinity?
- If identity is so important, then why can't boys choose to identify with hyper-masculinity even if they choose to identify as a female?
- What are the differences in the brains of adult women and men, and what roles do emotions have in connecting the two in relationships?
- Are men more vulgar today than women?
- Why do males and females appear as the most compatible in terms of relationships and are considered central toward the longevity of societal stability?

Informal Survey of Teachers

The following questions were posted on several social media pages, including Facebook groups and Reddit education threads, that feature teachers and education professionals. Below is a selection of revealing excerpted responses from teachers across the United States.

Questions Posted on Social Media Pages
1. What are your opinions on the allegations that public schools in America have become far too toxic to be effective?
2. What triggers school environments to become toxic in the first place, both in the classroom and around campus?
3. Can you suggest ways schools can solve the problems associated with toxicity?

Teachers' Responses
The following responses appear in no special order, and names have been removed for privacy.

- Toxicity is caused by administrations that micro-manage and do not give their staffs the respect they deserve!
- Principals that micro-manage are toxic. Any independent thinking is squashed in negative and nasty ways.
- Our administration is not really involved in the day-to-day workings of the staff and they are still toxic. We have cliques. One is known as the mean girl clique. You think teachers would know better.
- We had a weak principal and he finally left. He was replaced with an even weaker one and things got worse—more toxic. The weaker one

left only to be replaced by a friend of the district administrator and under this person things became toxic again. They do not even see it!
- We had a terrible principal and the students nicknamed him "Toxic Joe." It is safe to say that the toxicity is through the whole school.
- I agree that administrators can create toxic environments. The administrator I had last year was horrible and the school was very unsuccessful. However, this year my administrator was much better and what I saw a lot of was poor attitudes from teachers. It has to be a two way street. Teachers needs to know that not everything admin does is going to be accepted.
- We all want to feel appreciated. We all want to be recognized for our good work. That can be from administrators or other teachers. But much of the toxic climate comes from building leadership. Those leaders have to be willing to support excellence and root out mediocrity and inspire new thinking. Teachers have to feel safe enough to step out and share in their own buildings.
- Administrators that micro-manage and are unsupportive are part of the equation. Add in veteran teachers who don't willingly help or include newer staff members and it's a recipe for toxicity.
- Here is one thing that I struggle to understand. We expect our students to accept the challenge of learning new things, but some staff members want to stay comfortable doing things the way they've always done them. If you are not excited about learning, why would you choose to be an educator?
- I agree that a toxic gap widens when one-half of the staff is innovative and takes risks and the other one-half is set in their ways. The ones set in their ways resent the ones trying new approaches and actually get upset with them.
- We should not be made to feel like we are traitors if we continue to learn and grow.
- Too much negativity coming from the teachers. Turn it around as fast as you can. Mix up the groups in Professional Development. Don't let the cliques develop. Mix the young and old, inexperienced and experienced, introverts and extroverts, and content areas. Help teachers get to know one another and then encourage teachers to do the same in their classes with students.
- My school is very toxic, new principal feeds on the gossip and allows it to occur while saying there is no place for it. He does not micromanage. In fact I can never find him. He is never in his office.

- The principal at my school has been caught by janitors and teachers in compromising positions with female faculty members in rooms on campus. When brought to the attention of the district, nothing was done. His storied sexual advances have made our campus extremely toxic.
- I've been teaching for twenty-three years and this is the first year I've eaten alone. It was not like this years ago. A lot of teachers retired in the last five years. I'm now one of the old ones but I love technology and staying up-to-date. Things are just so different. The new teachers don't know how great it used to be years ago. We had a micro-managing principal swoop in for three years and do a lot of toxic damage. We got a new principal this year but he's got his work cut out for him to change things.
- The teacher across the hall makes our whole building toxic. We do our best to ignore her but sometimes she pulls us down.
- Fortunately, we have a great principal, which is a big change from the previous one. I call him a "yes man." I say that because he is open to anything we ask. We have bigger fish to fry than sweating a picture on a wall. If we want to try something he is all for it. He sets a positive tone, which is a far cry from the previous toxic principal.
- At times my school feels competitive. I'm not competitive at all and it's hard to work as a team when someone or everyone else thinks they have the right answer. Also, the more we complain the more toxic the school environment is. However, when teaching is so hard it's difficult not to air frustrations.
- Too many teachers are wanting to be The Bully.
- Toxicity starts at the top.
- Micro-managing and forgetting that teachers are professionals makes our school toxic.
- In my experience toxicity is always some form of bullying or control issues, usually from administration or a colleague.
- I think toxic environments start when the "right" combination of people and circumstances happen. The trick is seeing it and doing something about it!
- Teachers should not be the types to sit back and watch the train wreck, but rather get in there and get messy. We need to do the same with toxicity. We wouldn't wait until the first-year teacher is drowning to help him. We're in there day-one offering our help, stopping by to encourage when we know they've had a bad day. Why don't we do the same for others? Veteran teachers and administrators can have bad days, weeks, months, too. The real trick is knowing when to offer a shoulder to cry on, an ear to listen, and to just be there to help them when they ask.

- I've worked in cliquey schools, and dealt with the mean girls head on. It is a real problem when students see adults bullying other adults. It is never easy! But a simple smile, and "hi, how are you," goes a long way! We tell students not to be bystanders to bullying, we must demonstrate that we mean it! Be an up-stander and stand up to bullying!

Tackling Toxicity in Schools

While it is true that school-based emotional toxins poison people and controversies stir up emotions, schools must consider whether these realities are worth the cost to education on their campuses. The fact remains that addressing any toxic element at schools usually results in increased numbers of parents siding with whatever provides political advantage. A good example of political advantage is the restorative justice movement whereby students are kept on campuses when they commit offenses that would have previously resulted in suspension or expulsion.

There are political advantages in terms of increasing the rates of graduation, lowering possible incarceration rates, and increasing the confidences of current and future voters. However, the academic advantages realized are debatable.[33]

Whether inner-city schools, blue states or red states, and election year or not, children in America are in our schools and counting on our teachers and the various school systems to educate them and prepare them for their futures. But sometimes they rebel and for good reason.

Some students are using graduation ceremonies to their advantage. They expose the toxicity of their school, claiming it has been overlooked for too long.

A hefty price may be paid if students' graduation speeches go off script and embarrass the school administration and subject the audience to the toxic underbelly of the inner culture of the school. One such example occurred in Vancouver, Washington, when a senior gave a speech and went off script to reveal major problems with bullying and sexual assault and blamed the environment created by inept administrators. The student's claim was that many students were placed in very serious toxic environments. He reiterated that administrators' hands are often tied given the current laws that protect certain groups of people over others.[34]

In order to detox American public schools, there must be agreements to either allow freedom of speech and expression or to scale back everyone's freedom. There is no fairness in disallowing disagreement because it simply is not in keeping with current waves of social trends. This is where laws come into play.

Whenever politicians from one party have all the power to decide what speech is offensive—and legislate against this form of speech—their actions are deemed as toxic. Adding to this toxicity is the enforcement against the freedom of speech of one group while protecting the speech of another group. Government protecting people from the effects of speech while legislating an encasement of protections for those offended only inflames those who claim political bias.

All too often, what usually happens is that, for those whose speech is restricted, there are efforts to swing social pendulums to make up for incidents in the past. For example, those who are labeled as hateful to one group may themselves treat others hatefully through payback rhetoric and actions. This cannot be allowed to occur on school campuses.

Schools that would take seriously the detoxing of their institutions should consider working with parents and community-support groups along with law enforcement and clergy to address the following three major questions.

- Should schools be the places for social and moral activism for students or places of learning to apply knowledge and skills for the workplace? Can schools possibly focus on both and maximize effectiveness in preparing students for the twenty-first-century economy?
- What social issues exist today that are creating a toxic environment in schools and disenfranchising various student demographics and families?
- Why has academic urgency been compromised by social agency in our public schools, and should schools maintain any responsibility to adhere to the impossible task of educating the whole child?

Toxic teachers should be held accountable for their words and actions, but they cannot be held accountable if the school itself promotes or tolerates the very toxicity it says it deplores. This is where toxicity becomes deplorable: the overall school environment, inside and outside the classroom, froths with negativity. When teachers feel emboldened in their toxicity, one should look no further than the school principal to see whether such a culture is aligned with his or her leadership.

The accountability for toxicity at schools begins at the top. Weak administrators who allow teachers to run amok with little accountability also are evidence of the downturn of respect on campus. Where toxic schools exist, they are often allowed to continue under the leadership of a weak administrator's bad example of trying to please everyone. Weakness enables toxicity as much as bullying enables toxicity. The survey comments above illustrate the need for strong administrative leadership in public schools.

There must be a balance struck in working with diverse faculties and staffs. Walking on egg shells, as the phrase goes, around campus is an environment that causes teachers to shut their classroom doors and cloister away to do their jobs. There is often fear associated with parental phone calls and conferences. Some teachers hear the word *accountability* and immediately think something must be wrong.

To combat the toxic environment, there must be a beginning and an effort to move forward. School personnel should be allowed to take climate surveys anonymously. Districts should take part in visiting schools to determine the climate among faculty and staff. Teachers should feel free to share their feelings without repercussions, and private surveys are good ways to begin moving away from toxicity.

Obvious signs that toxicity is kept alive by the principal is chronic side taking, playing favorites, or talking behind the backs of his or her faculty, the school parents, or to district officials. Sometimes detoxing a school means reassigning a principal, breaking up a staff, or doing both.

Developing a Strategy to Detox Schools: It Begins at the Top

There are at least three repetitive refrains about school toxicity that appear throughout the list of teacher excerpts above. These include (1) toxicity can be injected into schools from the top down; (2) toxicity can be brought into schools from within by teachers, administrators, parents, and students; and (3) toxicity can be brought into public schools by a combination of both, from without and within the schools, including requirements from state and federal levels.

It is incumbent upon principals to set the tone for a school campus. As the reader will have noticed from the information in this chapter, toxicity stems from principals who micro-manage their schools. "Since principals are largely responsible for a school's culture, it can fall on them to do what they can to correct the situation."[35] Sometimes, it falls on principals to be the bad ones as they attempt to ferret out toxicity and remove the elements that are the causes. However, serious difficulties can arise when it is the principal's actions that are set in motion to correct his or her own administrative inactions. Consequently, the principal would find a dilemma over a conflict of approaches.

As long as there are education laws and education policy, teachers have had

> to comply with what they see as wrong-headed mandates—implementing teaching strategies or behavior management programs that they think will

best serve their students. But a new study by the *American Educational Research Journal* finds that some of these choices may be causing teachers moral harm—that is the feeling that they or their colleagues are making decisions that go against their deeply held values. In a survey of educators in an urban Midwest district, 4 in 5 said they witnessed other staff doing things that were morally wrong, while almost half said they themselves had acted in a way that betrayed their values.[36]

The term *moral injury* "was coined by military psychologists and psychiatrists, who found that post-traumatic stress disorder was too narrow a concept to capture some of the emotions that veterans experienced."[37] Erin P. Sugrue, author of the study, stated, "What they were finding is that there are plenty of vets who were troubled by things they had witnessed or things they had done that weren't directly related to their safety, per se, but were related to their belief in themselves as a moral person and the world as a moral place."[38] The framework of the study consisted of the following rating scale. "(1) Transgressions by others; (2) Transgressions educators committed themselves; and (3) Betrayal—feeling as if school leaders, colleagues, or education policymakers had betrayed educators or students."[39]

The majority of the teachers "felt that others in their schools or districts had committed moral wrongs. But teachers weren't faulting their colleagues. About 45 percent said that they themselves had acted immorally on the job."[40] Sometimes, teachers realize it is they who are creating a toxic work environment.

Whenever considering whether a school is toxic, there are certain factors that must be considered. Many of these have already been discussed in earlier chapters. But what is a good strategy to get to the root of a school's toxicity and begin to repair some of the damage done over time?

Angela Watson's focus, in her book *Unshakeable: 20 Ways to Enjoy Teaching Every Day . . . No Matter What*, is on teachers' mind-sets and moving beyond certain aspects of teaching that are points of frustration. Chapter 7 encourages teachers to do their part "to create a positive school culture."[41] Watson writes, "In my opinion, a culture of complaining is the most pervasive influence in schools. It starts with a handful of pessimistic teachers who only see the bad and get a kick out of telling newer teachers how much worse the school and profession have gotten over the years."[42] In efforts to thwart school toxicity, Watson asserts that teachers should limit their "emotional investment in negative coworkers."[43] She also gives teachers a positive vision and a way forward.

> A healthy work environment makes a tremendous difference in how much you enjoy teaching, and you deserve to be in a place where you feel supported and energized each day. If your school's morale is in the gutter and there is palpable

tension among faculty and administrators, please know that you are not powerless over that situation, no matter how much it might feel that way. You have the right to seek out other teaching opportunities . . . and you have the ability to influence the work environment at the school you're at right now. For any school dealing with toxicity on campus, or an extension of the school by way of activities, different areas of concern need to be analyzed. The interesting part of this analysis lies in the fact that the very origin of the issue and its solution may come from the same level of concern. The following list includes these levels of concern. Each of these levels of concern will include suggestions on how to ameliorate toxicity within it. . . . Don't give your power to a toxic administrator or allow other staff members' attitudes to determine whether you enjoy your work. . . . You, personally, can have tremendous influence on your work environment if you choose to exercise it. . . . Your attitude is the deciding factor in how much you enjoy your work, and you have the power to impact everyone round you with the choices you make.[44]

What follows are some suggestions on changing a school culture to a positive and encouraging teaching and learning environment. When your school is toxic:

- Develop a *positive outlook* on life and begin to see through the lens of promise and optimism. If you cannot find the mechanism to move into such a perspective, then latch on to someone whom you respect and who demonstrates a vibrant nature.
- Refuse to *compromise* your will and your optimism if the majority of teachers are negative and see students and parents as the basic problem in education.
- Demonstrate *the ability for humility* in sharing the goodness of other teachers and students. Do not view giving of oneself in this way as a weakness or some sort of loss of power. That conclusion is the result of an already toxic environment.
- Exercise a *welcoming spirit* and be willing to accept newer faculty, especially the young and energetic new teachers. Stay away from cliques or encouraging the newer teachers to join them.
- Practice *encouragement* and do not judge other teachers or administrators. Being a mentor to others means being a positive example.
- Balance *honesty with empathy* when difficult discussions take place. Practicing a bit of grace closes the gap between teachers and begins to lay the groundwork for positive relationships on campus.
- Avoid *tacit agreement* in toxic environments. Speaking up about something that is toxic might exacerbate a toxic environment. However,

tact and approach are hallmarks of healthy environments since these demonstrate respect for others. Remember that being quiet in the midst of toxicity may result in affecting students and parents in your classroom.
- Remember that *the ways teachers interact* with each other in front of students, parents, administrators, and so forth, will affect the way students view the teachers and their schools. Sarcasm is not always understood as something positive and should be avoided in front of students.
- Teachers should *practice the culture they want* to work in and with on campus. Therefore, develop a practical plan to instill the positive culture that is desirable at your school.
- Develop a *good reputation* that can hold others' conversations with you as private. Trust is an important feature among teachers and administrators on campuses of healthy schools. One of the first traits to nose-dive within toxic environments is trust in others. Remember that toxicity thrives in the midst of loose lips.

In closing, there is no perfect plan to detox American schools. As long as people are involved in the process, making positive gains could become messy. However, led by a caring and respected administrator, schools have a fighting chance to move forward toward health.

Healthy schools lead to healthy teachers and students, each of which is more than a social product. When it comes to students, futures are at stake—theirs and our nation's! For this reason, American education must recalibrate to understanding the urgency of academics as the focal point of our nation's public schools.

Notes

1. Elise Sole. "Teacher retires from 'toxic' profession in Facebook post: 'I will not miss what education has become.'" *Yahoo Lifestyle*. May 3, 2019. Retrieved from https://www.yahoo.com/lifestyle/teacher-retires-from-toxic-profession-in-facebook-post-i-will-not-miss-what-education-has-become-015939592.html.

2. Pernille Ripp. "When a school becomes toxic—What can we do to change school culture?" *Author Blog*. February 14, 2016. Retrieved from https://pernillesripp.com/2016/02/14/when-a-school-becomes-toxic-what-can-we-do-to-change-school-cultureul/.

3. Claire Groden. "Life-saving drugs." *CNN Health*. July 18, 2013. Retrieved from https://www.cnn.com/2013/07/18/health/toxin-treatments-time/index.html.

4. Staff. "Is your school's culture toxic or positive?" *Education World*. No date. Retrieved from https://www.educationworld.com/a_admin/admin/admin275.shtml.

5. Stephany Soto. "9 signs your school might be toxic." *Medium*. November 16, 2017. Retrieved from https://medium.com/@teamteachon/9-signs-your-school-might-be-toxic-a4caca5fd201.

6. Elise Sole. "Teacher retires from 'toxic' profession in Facebook post."

7. Ibid.

8. Valerie Strauss. "34 problems with standardized tests." *Washington Post*. April 19, 2017. Retrieved from https://www.washingtonpost.com/news/answer-sheet/wp/2017/04/19/34-problems-with-standardized-tests/?utm_term=.f432f169c842.

9. Ibid.

10. Ibid.

11. Herman, Reinke, and Hickman-Rosa, "Empirically derived profiles of teacher stress, burnout, self-efficacy, and coping and associated student outcomes." Cf. Tim Walker. "How many teachers are highly stressed? Maybe more than people think." *NEA Today*. May 11, 2018. Retrieved from http://neatoday.org/2018/05/11/study-high-teacher-stress-levels/.

12. Herman, Reinke, and Hickman-Rosa, "Empirically derived profiles of teacher stress, burnout, self-efficacy, and coping and associated student outcomes."

13. Ryan Prior. "Burnout is an official medical diagnosis, World Health Organization says." *CNN*. May 27, 2019. Retrieved from https://www.cnn.com/2019/05/27/health/who-burnout-disease-trnd/index.html.

14. Herman, Reinke, and Hickman-Rosa, "Empirically derived profiles of teacher stress, burnout, self-efficacy, and coping and associated student outcomes."

15. Amy Lynn Tompkins. "Principal hotline: Why is my boss so insensitive?" *School Leaders Now*. February 25, 2019. Retrieved from https://schoolleadersnow.weareteachers.com/principal-hotline-teacher-principal-communications/.

16. Herman, Reinke, and Hickman-Rosa, "Empirically derived profiles of teacher stress, burnout, self-efficacy, and coping and associated student outcomes."

17. Ibid.

18. Tim Walker. "How many teachers are highly stressed? Maybe more than people think." *NEA Today*. May 11, 2018. Retrieved from http://neatoday.org/2018/05/11/study-high-teacher-stress-levels/.

19. Colleen Clemens. "What we mean when we say, 'toxic masculinity.'" *Teaching Tolerance*. December 11, 2017. Retrieved from https://www.tolerance.org/magazine/what-we-mean-when-we-say-toxic-masculinity.

20. Ibid.

21. Ibid.

22. Ibid.

23. Ibid.

24. Ibid.

25. Joanna Schroeder. "8 things you must never do when raising boys." *Good Men Project*. July 28, 2017. Retrieved from https://goodmenproject.com/featured-content/things-you-must-not-do-when-raising-boys-hesaid/.

26. Ernest J. Zarra III. *Assaulted: Violence in schools and what needs to be done*. 2018. Lanham, Maryland: Rowman & Littlefield Publishers, pp. 21–41.

27. Andrew Pollack. "California's ban on school suspensions invites another Parkland." *National Review*. September 18, 2019. Retrieved from https://www.nationalreview.com/2019/09/california-ban-school-suspensions-invites-another-parkland/.

28. Camilla Turner. "Teachers are leaving school in groups for fear of 'violent repercussions from parents.'" *The Telegraph*. May 4, 2019. Retrieved from https://www.telegraph.co.uk/education/2019/05/04/teachers-leaving-school-groups-fear-violent-repercussions-parents/.

29. Ibid.

30. Staff. "Social media fact sheet." Pew Research Center. June 12, 2019. Retrieved from https://www.pewinternet.org/fact-sheet/social-media/.

31. Camilla Turner. "Teachers are leaving school in groups for fear of 'violent repercussions from parents.'"

32. Ernest J. Zarra III. *Assaulted: Violence in schools and what needs to be done.*

33. Frederique Autrin, Anatolia Batruch, and Fabrizio Butera. "Social justice in education: How the function of selection in educational institutions predicts support for (non)-egalitarian assessment practices." *Frontiers in Psychology*. June 4, 2015. Vol. 6: 707. Retrieved from https://www.ncbi.nlm.nih.gov/pmc/articles/PMC4454842/. Cf. Zachary Wright. "It's non-negotiable. We have to teach social justice in our schools." *Education Post*. December 4, 2017. Retrieved from https://educationpost.org/its-non-negotiable-we-have-to-teach-social-justice-in-our-schools/.

34. Kerry Justich. "Student barred from walking at graduation after accusing administrators of ignoring sexual assault, bullying at school." *Yahoo Lifestyle*. June 6, 2019. Retrieved from https://www.yahoo.com/lifestyle/student-barred-graduation-accusing-administrators-ignoring-sexual-assault-bullying-212343809.html.

35. Amelia Harper. "Toxic teachers present disciplinary challenges to administrators." *Education Dive*. October 22, 2018. Retrieved from https://www.educationdive.com/news/toxic-teachers-present-disciplinary-challenges-to-administrators/540102/.

36. Sarah Schwartz. "Teachers often experience 'moral injury' on the job." *Education Week*. May 23, 2019. Retrieved from https://blogs.edweek.org/teachers/teaching_now/2019/05/moral_injury_teachers.html.

37. Ibid.

38. Sarah Schwartz. "Teachers often experience 'moral injury' on the job." Cf. Erin P. Sugrue. "Moral injury among professionals in K–12 education." *American Educational Research Journal*. May 2019. Retrieved from https://www.scribd.com/document/413190105/Moral-Injury-Among-Professionals-in-K-12-Education#download.

39. Sarah Schwartz. "Teachers often experience 'moral injury' on the job." Cf. Erin P. Sugrue. "Moral injury among professionals in K–12 education."

40. Sarah Schwartz. "Teachers often experience 'moral injury' on the job."

41. Angela Watson. *Unshakeable: 20 ways to enjoy teaching every day . . . no matter what.* 2015. New York: Due Season Press and Educational Services, p. 91.

42. Ibid., pp. 91–92.

43. Ibid.

44. Ibid., pp. 91–93.

Index

Abington v. Schempp, 15
abortion, 2, 72
absolute, 38
abuse of teachers, 57–59; in Australia, 59–60; in the United Kingdom, 59; in the United States, 58–59
academic urgency, 8–9
accountability toward students, 61; teachers' frustration with, 61; wedges to, 61
action civics, 88–89
addictions among, 64; American society, 67; elementary schools, 64; high schools, 65; middle schools, 65
addiction to, 64; alcohol, 64; heroin, 64; marijuana, 64–65; pornography, 64; prescription drugs and opioids, 64; vaping, 64; violence, 64
addicts, 64
advocacy, xiv
Affordable Care Act (ACA), 63
AIDS, 88
air of arrogance, 108
Almighty, 5

alpha male, 112
Amante, Darnisa, 44
ambition, 3
American Federation of Teachers, 94
American Psychological Association (APA), 112
American Revolution, 14
Amiel, Henri-Frederic, 119
Answers in Genesis, 38
anti-bias training, 44
Anti-Defamation League (ADL), 26
anti-racism, 108
anti-Trump, 71
apathy, 10
Articles of Confederation, 15
Ash, Andrew, 30
Asians, 113
Aslan, Reza, 71
assassination, xv
Association for Supervision and Curriculum Development (ASCD), 114
atheists, 69
attitude of battletude, 94
anti-Christian bias, 18

Badass Teachers' Association (BAT), 94
Baldwin, James, 121
bias in the media, 18
bias, 18
biological essentialism, 144
Bob Jones University v. United States, 72
book banners, 121
boys, 145
need emotional guidance, 145; potentially toxic, 145
Boy Scouts of America (BSA), 73
Brady, Tom, 111
brain scans and gender differences, 40, 144
Branch Davidians, 4
Braunfield v. Brown, 15
Brice-Hyde, Jamy, 93
Brown v. Board of Education, 47
Burlington, Vermont, 62
Burton, Robert, 11
Bush, George W., 6, 13, 17
Buss, David, 12
Butler, Judith, 38

California, 4, 87
Calos, Rebecca, 119
Calvin College, 71
Campbell University, 71
Cantwell v. Connecticut, 15
Carroll, Jonathan, 137–140
Catcher in the Rye, 121
Cecil B. DeMille Award, 37
Center on Extremism, 26
Chait, Jonathan, 76
characteristics of toxic teachers, 93
charter schools, 7
Christian colleges and LBGTQ+, 71
Christian faith, 18
Christian heritage, 2
Christian teachers, 126
Christianity, 14–19, 33
Christophobia, 18–19

Church of Scientology, 4
civic activists, 8
civic participation, 8
Civil War, 2, 9
Claremont Colleges, 70
Clark, Georgia, 27
classrooms as mission fields, 34
Clemens, Colleen, 35–36, 143–145
Clinton Administration, 13
Clinton, Hillary, 26
CNN, 33
coarse language, 13
Cold War, 75
College Pulse survey, 77
Committee for Children, 88
Common Core, 6, 63, 114–115, 120–121
County of Allegheny v. ACLU, 16
cult of the individual, 5–6
cultural, 62
catalysts of activism, 61
elites, 62
hot button issues, 63
inputs, 11
culture; addicted to emotions, 27; changers, xiii, 5, 66; coarseness of, xv; neo-, xiii
of death, 9; of violence, 9; pejoratives in, xv; secularized, 19; stereotypes, 112
curriculum triggers, 122–123

Darling-Hammond, Linda, 6
demasculinization, 112
detoxing American schools, 137–141
Dewey, John, 6
DiAngelo, Robin. *See White Fragility*
diminishing student beliefs, 123
District of Columbia, 65
diversity training as toxic, 42
doxing, 30
drama, 68; after Supreme Court decisions, 68; by elitists, 69; in American culture, 68; in higher

education, 70; is cyclical, 73; of activism, 74; of ideology, 75; of political correctness; within social organizations, 72
driving under the influence, 65
drug epidemic, 8, 65
duck and cover drills, 75
dysphoria, 41
Duffell, Joan, 88

Eastern Mennonite University, 71–72
educators traumatize educators, 59
Edwards v. Aguillard, 16
Elk Grove v. Newdow, 17
emotional addicts, 27
emotional awakening, 5
emotional outcomes, 5
Engle v. Vitale, 15
entertainment icons, 5
Epperson v. Arkansas, 16
equity training, 44
Eurocentric, 19
European settlers, 14
Everson v. Board of Education, 15
Every Student Succeeds Act, 63
exclusive oneness, 5

factions, 2
fake news, 33
false doctrines, 4
family background, 63
Federalist 10, 2
federalists, xvi
feminists, 112,
Fields, Douglas, 12
fighting toxicity, 142; by remaining responsible, 142
through teacher recognition, 142; with an empathetic administrator, 142–143
Fine, Cordella, 38
First Amendment, 15, 35
First Corinthians, 12
flipped society, 29

Florida, 140; high stakes tests unreliability, 141; parents opt out of tests, 140–141; state assessments, 140
Fort Worth Independent School District, 27
Founding Fathers, 2
France, Paul, 125
free speech, 41
Fuller Theological Seminary, 72

Gates, Bill, 6
Gatestone Institute, 30
Gen Z, xiv, 27, 67, 118
gender, 63
gender differences between boys and girls, 143
God, 20
and His Word, 38
of love, 20; image of, 38
Golden Globes. *See* Cecil B. DeMille Award.
Golden Rule, xvii, 19
Goldhill, Olivia, 10
Google, 13
Go Tell it on the Mountain, 121
gynocentrism, 112–113;
Ham, Kenneth, 38
Harper, Amelia, 92
hatred of men, 112
hedonism, 20
Heritage Foundation, 41
Hillsdale College, 70
Hispanics, 113
HIV, 88
home schools, 7
homophobic, 18
homosexuality, 18
hostility toward police, 26
Howard, Tyrone, 44

identity movements, 29
illegal students, 27
Illinois, 4

implicit bias, 44
increase of violence in schools, 146
individual empowerment, 29
Individuals with Disabilities Education Act, 47, 117
indoctrination, 4
intolerance, xv
intoxicated, xiii
Islam, 17–18
Islamophobia, 17–18

Jones, Jim, 4
Jonestown, 4
Josephson, Allan M., 40
Judaism, 33
Judeo-Christian 14; principles, 14; values, 117

Korean War, 2
Kendi, Ibram, 108
killing, 9
Knight, Judy J. Z., 4
Knight Foundation, 77
Koresh, David, 4
Ku Klux Klan, 71
Kusz, Kyle, 111
Kutztown University, 35

learning styles, 63
Lee v. Weisman, 16
Lemon v. Kurtzman, 16
Les Miserables, 121
LGBTQ+, 33, 35, 38–41, 72, 112–113, 116, 123, 125–126; and the Nashville Statement, 72; and sex education curriculum, 87–88
Liang, Christopher, 111–112
Liberty University, 70
Lynch v. Donnelly, 16

Madison, James, xvi, 2, 3, 76, 83
MAGA, 33, 71
manhood, 112

manipulation of feelings, 86
Mansfield, Henry, 1
Mantell, Will, 44–45
marginalization, xv, 8, 108
Marsh v. Chambers, 16
masculinism, 112; hatred of, 112
viewed by feminists, 112
masculinity, 35–36
traditional, 112
under fire, 35–36
Massachusetts, 4
mass murders, 9
McCarthyism, 107
McClain, Shirley, 6
McDaniel v. Paty, 16
Men's Therapeutic Cuddle Club, 111
messiah, 4
Michigan State University, 26
Micro-aggressions, 42
Mill John Stuart, 1
Milner, H. Richard, 41
misogynistic, 18, 37
moral influence, xiv
moral injury, 154
Morrison, Toni, 121–123
Mueller v. Allen, 16
Mulvahill, Elizabeth, 85
Murray v. Curlett, 15
Muslims, 17–19, 74

name calling, xv
narcissism, 29
Nathanson, Paul, 112
National Crime Victimization Statistics, 30
National Education Association, 94
nationalism and terror, 70–71
neo-orthodoxies, 4
neo-toxic era, 48
new dangers, 66
New York City Department of Education, 44
No Child Left Behind, 6, 140

O'Hair, Madeline Murry, 69
Obama Administration, 6, 45, 63, 97
groundwork for election of Donald Trump, 26; policies, 26
racial boldness, 26
Obergefell v. Hodges, 17
Old Glory, 14
oppositional defiant disorder, 45

Palo Alto High School, 31
personal offenses, 31
school newspaper criticized, 31; student comparisons hurtful, 31
parents relationships with children, 66
Parks-Ramage, Jonathan, 71
passion, 3
pejoratives, 27–28
Peterson, Kent, 138
physical abuse, 122
Pittsburgh, Pennsylvania, 146
polarization, 8
political, xiv
political activism, xiv
political correctness and pronouns, 75, 117
political extremism, 26
political intoxicants, 27
politics, 34; of group destruction, 34; of personal destruction, 34
prayer as toxic, 69
Pride Month, 116
private schools, 7
progressives, xiv, 4, 75–76
public education, 29
Pullman, Joy, 120

Qu'ran, 18

race, 40–42, 63, 70, 72
Race to the Top, 6
racism, xvi, 2
racist, 9, 27, 28
Rajneesh, Bhagwan Shree, 4

Ramtha, 4
RAND Corporation, 146
recalibrating American education, 156
reengineering of male identities, 144
regions of the United States, 90
religion of White man, 19
religion, 19, 63
resegregation, 8
restorative justice, 6
revolutions, 66
Reynolds v. United States, 15
Richards, Doyin, 37
Robbins, Jane, 105, 120
Rocklin School District sex education, 87
Roe v. Wade, 3, 17

San Francisco, 4
Santa Fe v. Doe, 17
Sax, Leonard, 39–40
schools, 30; and culture, 99; as political agencies, 61; as social agencies, 61; as soft targets, 30; change from top down, 99
Seattle public schools, 115
Second Amendment, 13
selective toxicity, 31–32
self-pleasures, 20
self-worship, 5
September 11, 2001, xv, 17
sexism, 74
sexual abuse, 122
sexual orientation, 63
shamed, 29
Sherbert v. Werner, 15
shifting blame, 28
Silver, Debbie, 85–86, 98
smart phones, 30–31
social, 6, 109
agency, 109
extremism, 26
institutions, 73
justice, 6, 45

social activists, 68; and attire, 68 ; and immigration, 68; and prayer in schools, 68–69; and restroom policy, 68; and transgender, 68; favor abortion, 68; for same sex marriage, 2, 68
social media platforms, 13
social-emotional learning, 88–89, 118 and Goldie Hawn, 118; and religion, 118; as most comprehensive program, 119; positives and negatives of, 89; provides tools for students to fix problems, 120; supported by CASEL, 120
soul fluidity, 4
Soviet Union, 75
sponges of empathy, 92
status quo, 8, 31
Stone v. Graham, 16
strategy to detox schools, 153–156
Streep, Meryl, 37
stress levels in toxic school environments, 142
students' feelings mandated by government, 120
students under the influence (SUI), 86
Sugrue, Erin P., 154
supremacist propaganda, 26
Supreme Court, 15, 17, 69
systemic racism, 41–43

tackling toxicity, 151–152; accountability, 152; getting back to academics, 152
teachers, 7
as activists, 9
attrition, 7, 117; Evangelical Christian, 32
guard against labeling students, 91
manipulate students, 86; Orthodox Jewish, 32
shortages, 7
stress levels, 141; survey, 148–151

Tennessee v. Scopes, 17
Texas State University, 26
Thakkar, Jonny, 76–77
theories of mind, 11
Torcaso v. Watkins, 15
toxic, 8, 89, 90; administrators, 100; America, 9; beliefs, 9
bravery as, 62; conflicts, 17
conflicts, 87; cultural upheavals as, 17, 69; curriculum, 121
elitism, 4; free speech as, 40; gender identity as, 35; hopelessness, 10
indicators, 105–106
inequality as, 45; inputs, 10; issues, 109; marriage and family as, 34; masculinity and femininity as, 35–38; parents, 145; religion, 1; school environment, xiv, xvi, 116, 138, 141; schools, 138; self-proclamations, 74
special services as, 46
sports as, 47–49, 62; states as, 38
substances, 63
teachers, 96
teachings, 105, 107, 126–128, 130; thoughts, xvii; traditional marriage as, 18; traditional values as, 36–38; transgenderism as, 74, 107
winning as, 63
toxicity, 1, 12, 48, 63, 84; and false optimism, 117
and technology, 30; and the public education system, 140 ; and therapy, 77; around the world, 146; catalysts of, 12; effects upon students' brains, 98; in the workplace, 48
managing, 123; manifested, 84; of students, 86; political, 33; religious, 32; racial expressions, 71
toxic masculinity, 110–114, 143; derived from, 110; erroneous meaning, 111; meaning of, 110
toxic, 83, 91; administrations, 91; and an air of arrogance, 84, 89;

and cynicism, 94; and delinquents, 92; and disillusionment, 93; and emotional triggers, 92; and pessimism, 91–92; and sarcasm, 94; and the Good Men Project, 110; as gossiper, 95; as non-active, 97; as talking snakes, 91; causes of trauma, 97; characteristics of, 138; effects upon students, 97; general description of, 95; not bad teachers, 84; understanding of, 89
traditional American values, xvi, xvii, 75
transphobic, 74
traumas, 9, 57; emotional, 60–61; involving teachers, 59; pertaining to students, 57–59
tri-state region, 90
Trump, 13, 27, 33, 63, 70, 91; and toxicity, 26; as White Nationalist, 71; declares national emergency, 64; election as president, 13–14, 26
Trump v. Hawaii, 17
truth, 4, 31
Twitter, 27
type-A personalities, 90
tyranny, 34

umbrella of diversity, 45
United Kingdom, 116
United States Women's National Team (USWNT), 61
unity on issues, 128–129
University of California, 11, 38, 44, 71
Berkeley, 38
Los Angeles, 44
Riverside, 71

San Francisco, 11
University of Georgia, 70
University of Kansas, 47
University of Louisville, 40
University of Texas-Austin, 12
University of Virginia, 26

Vanderbilt University, 26
Vargas, Lauren, 95
veteran teachers, 85
Vice President Joe Biden, 96
Vice President Mike Pence, 96
Vietnam War, 2, 75
violence, 9–10
among women, 146; drivers of, 12; in competition, 146; jihadist, 17
triggers of, 12
voter registrations, 109

Walker, Tim, 143
Wallace v. Jaffree, 16
Warfield, Benjamin Breckinridge, 6
Watson, Angela, 154
Westside v. Mergens, 16
White fragility, 107–108
White supremacist groups, 71
Whole Child Education, 114; impossible to achieve, 115–116
missing spiritual components, 115–116
unreasonable expectations, 114–115
Wilson, Carv, 59
Wisconsin v. Yoder, 16
woke folk, 5
World Wars, 2

Young Katherine, 112

zero tolerance, 30

About the Author

Ernest J. Zarra III, PhD, is a retired assistant professor of teacher education at Lewis-Clark State College. Zarra has five earned degrees and holds the PhD from the University of Southern California in teaching and learning theory with cognates in psychology and technology. He is a former Christian College First Team All-American soccer player and a former teacher of the year for a prestigious California public school and was awarded the top student in graduate education from the California State University at Bakersfield, California.

Dr. Zarra has written thirteen books and more than a dozen journal articles and has designed professional development programs. He is a national conference presenter, former district professional development leader, adjunct university instructor, and a member of several national honor societies. He also participated as a speaker of the Idaho Speakers Bureau as well as being a presenter in the Lewis-Clark Presents program, bringing special topics to high school students.

Originally from New Jersey, he and his wife, Suzi, a retired California public school teacher, live in Washington State and enjoy spending time with family, which includes their first grandchild.

www.ingramcontent.com/pod-product-compliance
Lightning Source LLC
Chambersburg PA
CBHW030138240426
43672CB00005B/182